Teaching
for Thinking

Teaching
for Thinking

Fostering Mathematical
Teaching Practices
Through Reasoning
Routines

Grace Kelemanik

Amy Lucenta

HEINEMANN
Portsmouth, NH

Heinemann

145 Maplewood Avenue, Suite 300

Portsmouth, NH 03801

www.heinemann.com

Offices and agents throughout the world

The authors and publisher wish to thank those who have generously given permission to reprint borrowed material:

Figure 1–4: "Avenues of Thinking" from *Routines for Reasoning: Fostering the Mathematical Practices in All Students* by Grace Kelemanik, Amy Lucenta, and Susan Janssen Creighton. Copyright © 2016 by Grace Kelemanik, Amy Lucenta, and Susan Janssen Creighton. Published by Heinemann, Portsmouth, NH. Reprinted by permission of the Publisher. All Rights Reserved.

Figures 2–1, 3–5, 4–9, 5–2 through 5–4, 5–6 from Anne Porter, AMP Content Creation. Reprinted by permission of Anne Porter.

Acknowledgments for borrowed material continue on p. 172.

Library of Congress Control Number: 2021950045

ISBN: 978-0-325-12007-2

Editor: Katherine Bryant

Production: Vicki Kasabian

Interior and cover designs: Suzanne Heiser

Cover photograph: © Getty Images/Jorg Greuel

Typesetter: Shawn Girsberger

Manufacturing: Val Cooper

Printed in the United States of America on acid-free paper

1 2 3 4 5 VP 25 24 23 22 21

November 2021 printing

For Magdalene Lampert
Because teaching is learnable

And in honor of our parents,
John and Grace,
Bill and Kathy.

Contents

Preface

Our work together began when we were supporting teachers to understand what the mathematical thinking summarized in the Common Core State Standards for Mathematical Practice looks like and sounds like. As we embarked on the work of unpacking the SMPs for ourselves and engaging teachers with them, we feared that only some students would have access to developing this kind of thinking. So, we designed and implemented instructional strategies that would support and engage a wide range of learners. When teachers applied the same strategies in their classrooms, they marveled that students engaged who previously hadn't, that the amount and quality of student discourse increased, and that students were able to articulate their mathematical thinking. Our work collided with Magdalene Lampert's work with "instructional activity structures" (Lampert and Graziani 2009; Lampert et al. 2010), and we began explicitly naming the elements we kept the same each time and the teacher moves embedded in them. Through this work, we developed a series of instructional routines that we call reasoning routines. We introduced four of these routines in our previous book, *Routines for Reasoning: Fostering the Mathematical Practices in All Students* (2016), and present new ones in this book.

We have often had the privilege of stepping into teachers' classrooms as they continued to learn routines through coaching, learning labs, videos, or teacher reflections. Although teachers learned the flow of the routine relatively easily, "teaching for thinking" was often a new approach for teachers, challenging their deeply ingrained teaching habits. We learned quickly that continued work within a reasoning routine provided teachers repeated opportunities to build new habits. We facilitated rehearsals of the routines, coaching sessions, and learning labs so that teachers could use the reasoning routines to focus on student thinking, step out of the middle, and support productive struggle. Through that work, we found that the instructional strategies integrated in the routines to support all students also served as concrete ways for teachers to work on their own practice. Likewise, coaches and district leaders realized the power that reasoning routines hold to develop equitable teaching practices within a department, school, or district.

About This Book

There are five essential teaching strategies that drive this work, and they serve as a unifying thread woven throughout the book. In Chapters 1 and 2, we name these strategies and the shifts necessary for teaching for thinking. Chapters 3 and 4 introduce two reasoning routines and highlight the embedded essential strategies. In Chapter 5, we pull back the curtain to share the process for developing a reasoning routine integrating these strategies. Finally, in Chapter 6, we share activities to work on the essential strategies to build habits of teaching for thinking.

We encourage you to start by reading Chapters 1 and 2. You may then choose a few different paths. If you are already familiar with one of our reasoning routines, you may want to explore Chapter 6 for activities to further your practice within that routine. Or, you could read either Chapter 3 (Decide and Defend) or 4 (Contemplate Then Calculate) to dive into a new reasoning routine. When you are ready, you could continue by reading Chapter 5 to design your own reasoning routine and read about how we designed our newest routine, Analyzing Contexts and Models. Regardless of your approach to reading this book, we hope you all explore Chapter 6 at some point so that you are ready to dig into the ways the routines can build your professional learning as well as develop your students' mathematical thinking and reasoning.

Acknowledgments

The content of this book is the product of our many learnings from many individuals and professional experiences along the way. Magdalene Lampert has been influential in our learning about routinizing mathematical experiences for students and for leveraging those routine experiences to develop teacher practice. We are beyond grateful for Magdalene's keen insight, her steadfast commitment to simplifying the complexities of teaching for thinking, and her championing of this work to benefit all students in all classrooms.

We acknowledge and deeply appreciate the many individuals and organizations who were instrumental in developing the instructional routines in this book. The resultant routines and ideas around working with them are clearer and stronger as a result of these collaborations. In particular, we thank the residents and collaborating teachers at the Boston Teacher Residency for supporting the development of Contemplate then Calculate; Kelly Hagan, her special educator colleagues, and her students at Wayland Middle School for opening their classroom door repeatedly to test-drive Decide and Defend; and Donna Sorila and her students and colleagues at Jonas Clarke Middle School for engaging in and providing feedback around Analyzing Contexts and Models. Finally, we thank the staff and attendees of the Teachers Development Group Leadership Seminar for their participation in the process of developing Decide and Defend and Analyzing Contexts and Models.

We acknowledge Anne Porter of AMP Content Creation for working with us to capture complex ideas around essential teaching strategies and designs for interaction with simple visuals and infographics that benefit students and teachers alike.

Thank you to the Heinemann team for their support of this project—particularly during a pandemic! Thanks especially to Josh Evans for answering our every question and maintaining a sense of humor from start to finish.

We literally would not have finished this book without our editor, Katherine Bryant! Not only did Katherine provide critical feedback on multiple drafts, but she educated us so well that we heard her voice in our heads as we were writing. We continue to be grateful for her work.

Teaching for Thinking

If we are to prepare our students for the increasingly complex and rapidly changing world they will inherit, we must teach them to think and reason mathematically. This is our greatest teaching challenge—not because students can't learn to think mathematically, but because we struggle to teach in ways that privilege thinking and provide support for struggling students. To do so often means breaking some of our more deeply rooted teaching habits. But if we want to change how students think about math, we need to change those habits.

Teaching for Mathematical Thinking

Our students face a data-drenched, constantly changing world in which new and more powerful technologies pop up with increasing frequency. They will need to tackle unpredictable problems instigated by technologies that don't exist today, using tools yet to be invented. Tackling complex problems in our students' future will require a range of expertise and variety of perspectives, and thus demand collaboration. Students who spend the bulk of their K–12 experience memorizing math and practicing procedures that ubiquitous smartphones and smart speakers can recall and calculate will not be prepared for their future. To be prepared, students must learn how to make sense of unfamiliar problem situations and persevere through their solutions. This will include being able to choose—and often learning how to use—appropriate tools to bring to bear on the problem, to work and communicate clearly with others to solve it, and to convince themselves and others that their approaches are sound and their results are correct. Said simply, our students need to be able to think and reason mathematically.

Learning Experiences to Teach Thinking

For students to develop as math thinkers, they need regular opportunities to make sense of and grapple with meaty math problems, time to think, and collaborative structures within which to work (National Council of Teachers of Mathematics 2014). If we give students a problem and they immediately know how to solve it, it is not a problem; it's an exercise. They are not learning to think and reason, they're developing fluency. Therefore, if students are to grow their math thinking, they must spend more time in math class bumping up against nonroutine math tasks. Research tells us that providing students with a steady diet of high-demand tasks leads to greater learning gains (Stein, Grover, and Henningsen 1996; Stein et al. 2009). Doing so also regularly positions students to develop math thinking practices.

This thinking and reasoning takes time. You cannot reason fast. You must read and reread the problem, pause to interpret its meaning, consider what might be mathematically important in the situation, clarify the question you are answering, question the assumptions you are making, represent the problem situation, consider possible approaches, and choose one that has promise. All this happens before actively executing your problem-solving plan, maintaining oversight, and convincing yourself of the validity of your solution.

All this work should be done in collaboration with others. Working collaboratively allows for the consideration of more perspectives, more processing space, and more opportunities to communicate your thinking, critique another's mathematical reasoning, and construct mathematical arguments. Collaboration not only leads to more effective sense making and problem solving and more accurately captures the way in which students will work "out in the real world," it positions students to develop critical math thinking practices. In sum, student learning opportunities must include cognitively demanding math tasks that promote thinking and reasoning, time to think, and collaborative structures within which to work.

Mathematical Thinking in Action

Let's take a look at Mr. Ryan's sixth-grade lesson for one example of what one such learning environment might look like. (This is an example of the Connecting Representations routine that we introduced in our first book, *Routines for Reasoning* [Kelemanik, Lucenta, and Creighton 2016], but you don't need to know the details of that routine to understand what happens in this lesson.) As you read over the vignette, reflect on Mr. Ryan's teaching. What do you notice? What do you wonder?

Like many middle school teachers, Mr. Ryan had seen far too many of his students "forget" to multiply every addend when distributing. For example, when working with an expression like $3(x + 6)$, students would often distribute the 3 and arrive at the incorrect expression $3x + 6$. To address this common error while encouraging mathematical thinking, Mr. Ryan provided his students with a task that positioned them to interpret a distributable expression by connecting it to a visual representation. This requires students to make sense of and connect the mathematical structure of an algebraic expression and a visual representation of that expression. He chose the task shown in Figure 1–1.

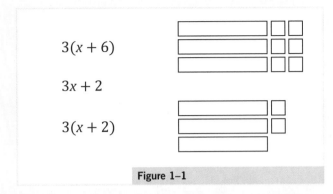

$3(x + 6)$

$3x + 2$

$3(x + 2)$

Figure 1–1

Today, Mr. Ryan explained, they would be connecting algebraic expressions to visuals by chunking and connecting to math they knew. He unveiled the set of three expressions and two visuals (as shown in Figure 1–1) and gave students several seconds of individual think time to orient to the representations, prompting them to ask themselves, "What part of the *visual* will help me connect to a chunk of the *expression*?" and "What about the *expression* will help me connect to the *visual*?"

He then told students to work with their partner to connect each visual with a different expression, projecting and explicitly prompting them to use one of two sentence frames to begin their discussion—"I noticed _____ so I looked for _____" or "_____ connects to _____ because _____." As pairs talked, Mr. Ryan circulated, listening in on their thinking. Based on what he was hearing, he decided which connection he wanted the class to discuss first and gave one partnership a heads-up that he would be asking them to present. Pulling the class back together, he called up the duo and reminded them that one would speak and the other would point: the pointer would point to the representations while their partner talked so that the class could follow along. He reminded the speaker to begin by using the sentence frame "We noticed _____ so we _____" and reminded the rest of the class to listen carefully and be prepared to rephrase the connection they heard using the sentence frame "They noticed _____ so they _____."

The speaker began, "We noticed that the first visual had three rows and all three rows had one rectangle and two squares, so we looked at the expressions to try to find one that was three groups of the same thing." The pointer pointed to each row in the first visual. The students continued, saying they decided that the last expression connected to the first visual because it had three "*x* plus twos" and the *x* was the rectangle and the two was the two squares. Mr. Ryan asked another student to rephrase the connection using the sentence frame "They noticed _____ so they _____." As the student rephrased, Mr. Ryan annotated the image, highlighting the student's thinking. He then checked with the partnership to see if the rephrase and annotation accurately captured the students' thinking. When they agreed, he pointed to the third expression and asked, "Where are the parentheses in the first visual?" He paused to give students time to think, and then prompted them to talk with a partner. After listening as they talked, he pulled the group back together and called on a specific student to share. The student said, "It's three times the parenthesis x plus two. So, the parentheses tell you what you are multiplying by three . . . what you have three of and the visual has three of the same rows, so my partner and I think the parentheses are like the rows." While they shared, Mr. Ryan pointed, and then, as he did before, asked another student to rephrase the idea, and annotated the representations to highlight what the student was saying (see Figure 1–2).

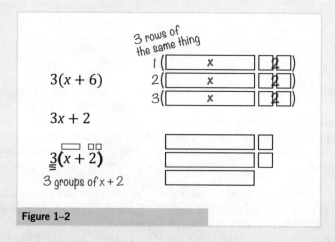

Figure 1–2

Mr. Ryan drew students' attention to the second visual and asked them to consider which of the remaining expressions connected to it. After pausing a few seconds, he instructed students to work with their partner to make the connection. The partners went back to work, and the class repeated the process of students sharing and rephrasing each other's ideas, the teacher annotating, and further reflection and discussion. To continue the discussion, Mr. Ryan asked, "What do we have three of in this expression?" and had the students turn and talk. He pulled them back after several seconds and a student shared, "We have three groups of x in this expression, not x plus two because there are no parentheses." Prompted by Mr. Ryan, another student added on, "We agree. You can tell by looking at the visual, the only thing you have three of are the rectangles, and then the two squares are separate. They're the plus two."

At this point, Mr. Ryan decided it was a good time to stop and have the students reflect. He reminded students that they were connecting representations to learn how to think mathematically and that meant learning what was important to pay attention to when they interpreted mathematical representations and learning useful questions to ask themselves. He projected three sentence frames (see Figure 1–3) and asked students to pick one and complete it in writing and then share what they wrote with their partner. He circulated and selected three reflections to share with the whole class. As students shared, Mr. Ryan made a public record of their reflections.

Meta-Reflection

A. When interpreting a *visual / expression*, I learned to pay attention to…

B. When connecting representations, I learned to ask myself…

C. A new mathematical connection I made was…

| Figure 1–3 |

- When interpreting an expression, I learned to pay attention to *parentheses because they will show me I have a group of something*.
- When interpreting expressions and visuals, I learned to ask myself, *Are there groups? And what's in each group?*
- When interpreting expressions and visuals, I learned to ask myself, *What's in each group?*

Key Features of Learning to Think Mathematically

What did you notice in this example? We notice three elements of Mr. Ryan's teaching that reflect three key aspects of how students learn to think mathematically: students think and reason, they have plenty of time to do so, and they work collaboratively.

Students are thinking and reasoning mathematically during Mr. Ryan's lesson. They make sense of and connect two different types of representations. The teacher does not show or explain to students how to make the connections, nor is there a well-rehearsed procedure for doing so. Although the teacher does orient students to the task at hand by offering "ask-yourself questions" to prompt thinking, the students are the ones interpreting the representations, comparing and contrasting them, deciding what might be mathematically important features, and then using what they are noticing to connect two different representations. Although there is a "right answer," students are determining, explaining, and justifying each connection in a variety of ways—all the stuff of math thinking and reasoning.

The second element of a learning experience that promotes thinking and reasoning is time to think. Students spend the bulk of the lesson working on one multistep task—connecting two visuals to two algebraic expressions. Students have time to think and process individually as they make sense of the representations as well as the ideas of their classmates. In addition, students have multiple opportunities to process ideas and thinking with a partner before sharing in the full group. Finally, students have time at the end to reflect on what they have learned about thinking mathematically.

Thirdly, the learning experience promotes collaborative sense making. Students do the bulk of their thinking and reasoning with a partner. Individual think time is relatively short and used to "ready" students for productive thinking with a partner. Students listen carefully to their classmates and regularly rephrase each other's thinking during full-group discussions. Finally, students make sense of and dig into peers' ideas that are shared in the full group when they engage in turn-and-talks.

Teaching Practices to Foster Mathematical Thinking

If teaching thinking requires specific student learning experiences, it would follow that it also requires certain teaching practices. The challenge in shifting to such practices does not lie in their complexity, but rather in the fact that they fly in the face of many of our current teaching habits that have been honed five periods a day, 180 days a year for years. They are second nature; we do them without even thinking. They include large grain-size routines like "I do, we do, you do," and small moves like repeating what a student says when it is important or correct.

These teaching practices are not inherently bad; they are simply ineffective tools for the job of developing math thinking and reasoning. Having students check their answers with a partner makes a lot of sense if the goal is for students to accurately execute a procedure. But if the goal is thinking and reasoning, shifting the focus away from the answer and toward the initial sense making of the problem is the way to go. Asking individual students questions during whole-class discussions is an effective move if you are assessing recall of previously learned information, but if the question requires students to chew on an idea, a turn-and-talk is a better move.

Developing teaching practices that support math thinking and reasoning will require us to make three critical shifts in our instruction:

- Focus on thinking: Shift time and attention away from answers and steps taken and place more focus on the underlying thinking and reasoning.
- Step out of the middle: Shift away from teacher-to-student interactions and toward student-to-student interactions.

- Support productive struggle: Shift teacher supports away from hints and suggestions and toward instructional designs that build students' capacity to struggle productively.

Let's unpack each of these shifts.

Shift 1: Focus on the Thinking

We need to spend more class time focusing on the thinking instead of the answers if our students are to become powerful math thinkers. We are not saying that arriving at a correct answer is not important; rather, we are saying that spending copious amounts of class time sharing answers and walking through calculations step by step will not help students learn to think and reason. To develop math thinking, we need to focus attention and classroom conversation where the thinking lives; namely, in what you pay attention to, the questions you ask yourself, and the subsequent actions you take.

Avenues of Thinking

In *Routines for Reasoning* (Kelemanik, Lucenta, and Creighton 2016) we highlighted three distinct avenues of mathematical thinking found in the Common Core math practice standards (i.e., quantitative reasoning, structural thinking, and repeated reasoning). We argued that if students developed these three avenues of thinking, they would have three ways into and through prickly math problems, and that flexibly using these avenues would lead to their problem-solving perseverance. The table in Figure 1–4 (on p. 8) from *Routines for Reasoning* articulates what a math doer pays attention to and asks themselves as well as the actions they take when thinking quantitatively, structurally, or through repetition.

To develop these avenues of thinking, we have to highlight and discuss them during lessons. Let's take a look at when in those lessons it's most effective to focus on the thinking.

Key Times to Focus on Thinking

There are three high-leverage points in a lesson to focus on thinking—when posing a problem, when discussing solutions, and when reflecting on learning.

Mathematical thinking and reasoning begin when a problem is posed and students first start making sense of it. Focusing on the thinking at this juncture in the lesson requires allowing time for students to grapple with making sense of the problem without stepping in to reword or explain it to them. It may even mean leaving off the actual question or covering up the numbers so that students cannot jump to solving the problem. It then requires actively orienting students to the thinking and pausing to highlight some of their initial thoughts before transitioning to leveraging that thinking to solve the problem.

Avenues of Thinking: A Framework for Making Sense of Several CCSS Standards for Mathematical Practice

Reason Abstractly and Quantitatively (MP2)	Look for and Make Use of Structure (MP7)	Look for and Express Regularity in Repeated Reasoning (MP8)
Attend to . . . Quantities and relationships	**Attend to . . .** The organization or behavior of number and space	**Attend to . . .** Repetition in processes or calculations
Ask Yourself • What can I count or measure? • What quantity or relationship does this number describe? • How do the quantities relate to each other? • How much bigger/smaller (how many times bigger/smaller) is one quantity than another? • How can I represent this situation so that I can see the quantities and relationships? • How can I show how much bigger/smaller (how many times bigger/smaller) one quantity is in my diagram? • What quantities or relationships do I see in the diagram? • Is there a "hidden" quantity or relationship that I can now see in the representation? • What does this (expression, variable, number, shaded region, etc.) represent in the problem context?	**Ask Yourself** • What type of problem is this? • Does this remind me of another problem situation? • How is this (situation, object, process, etc.) behaving? Can I connect it to something else I know? • What are the parts (chunks) of the process? • How can I get the answer without doing all the calculations? • How can I use properties to uncover structure? • How can I change the form of this (number, expression, shape) to surface the underlying structure?	**Ask Yourself** • Is there something in this problem context that repeats or suggests some regularity? • How can I create or use a repeated process to help me figure out what's going on in this problem? • What was my process? Was it the same every time? • Am I counting/drawing/building/calculating in the same way each time? • What about this process is repeating? • How can I describe the repetition in words/variables, etc.? • What operations can I use to model this process? • How can I use the repetition to make my rule?
Take Action • Determine which quantities/relationships are important • Identify quantities explicitly mentioned in the problem situation • Identify implied quantities • Use representations to see quantities and relationships • Decontextualize the problem situation • Contextualize the problem	**Take Action** • Chunk complicated mathematical objects (expressions, shapes, etc.) • Connect representations • Change the form of the number, expression, space (e.g., create equivalent expressions) • Recall and use properties, rules of operations, and geometric relationships	**Take Action** • Try several numbers and observe the process • Draw or build the next several figures in the series • Record and track calculations • Generalize the repetition

Figure 1-4

One way to orient students to the thinking is to have them first notice what might be mathematically important about the problem and/or context and then share some of their noticings in the full group. This will help students develop their mathematician's eye. Mr. Ryan helped students make sense of the set of representations he asked them to connect by posing two questions for them to ask themselves: "What part of the *visual* will help me connect to a chunk of the *expression*?" and "What about the *expression* will help me connect to the *visual*?" He then had students talk with a partner using a sentence frame ("I noticed _____ so I looked for _____"), which explicitly prompted them to share their initial thinking. Whether highlighting noticings or posing questions mathematicians often ask themselves, the goal is the same: to get students to pause and make sense and to become aware of and articulate their thinking.

Discussing solutions provides another opportunity to focus on thinking. Instead of having students state their answer and show what they did, shift the focus and have students start by sharing what they noticed or knew and how that helped them to approach the problem. This will likely feel unnatural to students who have spent years sharing and checking answers. It will require explicitly prompting students to share their thinking, and you will likely have to remind them again when they begin with an answer. Mr. Ryan helped his students focus on beginning with their thinking by posting and having them use the sentence frame "We noticed _____ so we _____." Additionally, he explicitly prompted the rest of the class to listen for the thinking, by telling them he would call on students to rephrase using the sentence frame "They noticed _____ so they _____." Knowing a classmate's answer or what they did will not help a student on future math problems, but learning what others are noticing and how that helps them make sense of and approach a problem will. Therefore, in thinking classrooms, the emphasis is not on what the student did, but on how they even knew to do what they did and how they knew they were right.

When focusing on mathematical thinking, it is critical that students take the time to reflect on and articulate what they are learning in terms of thinking like a mathematician. This includes identifying what they or their classmates pay attention to in math problems, contexts, and representations and which of those noticings turn out to be mathematically important. It also includes becoming aware of productive questions to ask when making sense of and doing mathematics. Mr. Ryan took time after his students connected expressions and visuals to have them reflect on their thinking. He provided three sentence frames ("When interpreting _____, I learned to pay attention to _____," "When connecting representations, I learned to ask myself _____," and "A new mathematical connection I made was _____") to focus their meta-reflections on the thinking. These meta-reflection prompts should focus on critical aspects of mathematical thinking. In this case they surface features of an algebraic expression, diagram, graph, or other mathematical object that will help students interpret those types of mathematical objects in the future. They should also result in the articulation of productive questions students can ask and answer to provide traction into future math problems and concepts. If we are going to teach students how to think and reason mathematically, we have to name the thinking and not just assume students are learning how to think mathematically because they worked on a cognitively demanding math task.

Focusing on student thinking sends the message to students that their ideas have merit, and students start to see themselves as capable mathematicians. Focusing on the thinking requires more than giving students hard math problems to solve. It means explicitly prompting and highlighting the thinking. The greatest challenge for us in doing so is to get out of the habit of asking for answers and into the habit of pressing for noticings and wonderings. The greatest challenge for students is to curb the compulsion to calculate and develop a need to know how they and their classmates are thinking. As students learn what to pay attention to and what to ask themselves, they will have avenues into pesky math problems and ways to make sense of complicated math content. They will become confident in their math doing and capable of applying the math they know to the problems in their world.

Shift 2: Step Out of the Middle

Teaching mathematical thinking requires us to step out of the middle and orient students to each other, so they can consider and collaborate around their mathematical ideas. Stepping out of the middle shifts the mathematical authority in the room. Instead of the teacher being the conduit of all math knowledge, students take on the responsibility of co-constructing their math understandings. Practically speaking, it means transforming teacher–student interactions into student–student interactions. When the teacher steps out of the middle, students work together to make sense of mathematics, solve problems, and convince themselves of the correctness of their work. When these collaborative work structures are set, the teacher's role shifts and they listen in on student conversations, select and sequence ideas to bring to the full group, and pose questions for students to chew on together. In this way new roles form—students become increasingly responsible for the mathematical thinking and teachers become increasingly responsive to their students' mathematical thinking.

Stepping out of the middle of students' math doing requires actively positioning students to attend to, take up, and work with each other's ideas. So, when teachers pose questions in a thinking classroom, instead of asking individual students to respond, they often prompt a turn-and-talk so that all students have a chance to think about the question as well as work though the language they will use in response. Rather than further explain a student connection, Mr. Ryan posed a question about that connection and prompted students to turn and talk to dig deeper into it. He then proceeded to tour the room, listening to get a sense of the range of student thinking, and avoided getting caught in a series of teacher–student interactions or conferring with each partnership.

The Role of Partners and Collaboration

In thinking classrooms, the bulk of the mathematical heavy lifting takes place in partnerships. Pairs, rather than small groups, allow for all students to be working on and talking about the math. Collaborative sense making is not working on a problem individually and then checking the answer with a partner. Co-constructing math knowledge means working together with a partner to make sense of and solve problems. Students must explain their thinking and also work to understand the reasoning of their partner. When pairs work together, two lines of thinking quickly become one as partners share ideas, select promising avenues of thinking, and together work to solve problems.

Because all students are talking, partner work also allows teachers to know the range of thinking in the room. We can hear how students are making sense of the task at hand and get a sense of the thinking underlying their written work. Mr. Ryan sent pairs off to connect representations and then circulated, listening in as partners shared what they noticed about the representations and worked together to make connections. He monitored their conversations and made decisions about which connections to share and who would share the connections, in what order. Once again, collaboration positions the teacher to be responsive to students' mathematical thinking.

When we step out of the middle, we may need to help our students learn to listen to their classmates. Mr. Ryan did that by previewing for his students that he would be calling on them to rephrase connections their classmates presented, and instead of underscoring what students shared, he regularly asked students to rephrase their classmate's ideas.

Shifting Authority

When teachers step out of the middle and students work together, students naturally begin to take responsibility for the validity of their ideas. As student pairs work together, they generate ideas, ask clarifying questions to better understand their partners' thinking, weigh the merits of multiple approaches, and convince themselves and each other of the soundness of their reasoning. As they prepare to share their thinking with others, they work together to clearly articulate, support, and justify their reasoning. Rather than looking for confirmation from their teacher, students evaluate their own work and seek to convince their classmates.

Stepping out of the middle and orienting students to each other sounds simple enough, but initially can be challenging. As teachers, we will need to reprogram ourselves not to repeat or rephrase student ideas and instead ask students to revoice their classmates' ideas. When we revoice, we step back into the middle and send the tacit message to students that they don't need to listen to each other, because if the idea is important, we will repeat it. Additionally, we must take care not to get caught in back-and-forths with a single student during full-group discussions, but rather engage the entire class in the idea through a turn-and-talk. Students may also have to recalibrate what it means to work with a partner and push back on their natural instinct to look to the teacher for answers.

Shift 3: Support Productive Struggle

Helping our students develop into powerful math thinkers means fighting the impulse to step in and rescue them as soon as they start to struggle. It means sending the message to students that mathematical thinking takes time and multiple passes to develop. Rather than providing hints and suggesting strategies so that students know the correct set of calculations to perform to get the answer, we must instead get in the habit of providing processing time and structures students can leverage to keep thinking productively about the task at hand. Our motivation to jump in quickly and lessen student struggle is well intentioned when we want to keep students from disengaging or getting frustrated or to ensure their problem-solving experience is a positive one. However, every time we do, we rob students of the opportunity to think and reason, and we send another subtle message that they are not capable of doing math themselves. Getting stuck is part of the thinking process and a necessary condition for developing perseverance.

Supporting productive struggle often means providing a variety of structures through which students can process ideas and thinking. Some examples of this are providing individual think time to prepare students to work with a partner or time to process an idea with a partner before sharing in the full group. Regularly asking students to rephrase classmates' ideas during full-group discussions provides struggling students multiple opportunities to hear and process the ideas the class is developing.

Thinking Takes Time

Providing time for students to make sense of a problem is especially critical. In thinking classrooms, students are given time to read a word problem multiple times, each time mining it for different information (e.g., context, question, important information). Mr. Ryan, for instance, purposely gave students time to interpret the representations before having them make connections with their partner. Students who do not have a clear sense of the problem context and what the question is asking often shut down before trying to solve the problem.

A less obvious place to make time for thinking is when students show and explain their work. It is critical to provide students time to consider a classmate's written work before that classmate starts explaining.

Supporting productive struggle sends the critical message to students that math thinking takes time and that they are capable mathematicians and can make progress when given space to think. As with the other shifts, supporting productive struggle will likely require pushing back against some deeply ingrained teaching habits like stepping in to explain and provide hints when students get stuck.

We expect you are now wondering, *How do I change the way I teach to place more emphasis on the thinking, facilitate more collaborative sense making, and support productive struggle for every student?* The answer lies in leveraging the predictable design and repeatable nature of reasoning routines, to which we turn next.

REFLECT ON YOUR READING

1. What do you think is *most* important about students learning to think and reason mathematically? Explain.

2. In this chapter we make the case that for students to develop as math thinkers, they need regular opportunities to make sense of and grapple with meaty math problems, time to think, and collaborative structures within which to work. Reflect on students' learning experiences in your classroom (or in classrooms you are familiar with); are they made up of these three ingredients? How frequently? If so, give examples. If not, which ingredient would you like to incorporate first? Why?

3. In this chapter we discussed three shifts in instruction required to foster mathematical thinking: focusing on thinking, stepping out of the middle, and supporting productive struggle. In what ways does your practice align with each of these shifts? What challenges or barriers do you expect to face in making the shifts? Which shift do you think would make the largest impact for your students' thinking?

The Power of
Reasoning Routines

The question is not whether all students can succeed in mathematics but whether the adults organizing mathematics learning opportunities can alter traditional beliefs and practices to promote success for all.

—National Council of Teachers of Mathematics, *Principles to Actions*

Instructional routines are powerful vehicles for developing mathematical thinking and teaching practices. Their predictable design and repeatable nature make routines habit inducing, and over time those habits coalesce into a deliberate practice. We created our reasoning routines to develop specific mathematical practices in all students. It turns out those same routines also bring about change in mathematics teaching practices. In this chapter we reintroduce our routines for reasoning and how they are designed to create a collaborative learning environment that places a premium on mathematical thinking and reasoning. We then talk about five essential strategies woven into the fabric of the routines that can be leveraged to make the three shifts in practice necessary for teaching all students to think and reason mathematically (i.e., shifting more focus on to the thinking, stepping out of the middle, and supporting productive struggle).

What Are Reasoning Routines?

Teachers use many different types of routines in the classroom to support student learning. From management routines like clock buddies and daily bell ringers that keep students following the group plan to discourse routines like think-pair-share and stop-and-jots that support class discussions, all these routines have the same thing in common: they leverage the predictability of their design and their repeated nature to build effective habits of learning. Our reasoning routines, which are designed to develop mathematical practices in all students, are no different. The predictability of the designs for interaction in our reasoning routines frees up brain space so that students can use more of their brain power thinking and reasoning mathematically. Over time and with repeated use students develop powerful mathematical habits of thinking.

We introduced four reasoning routines in *Routines for Reasoning*: Capturing Quantities, Connecting Representations, Recognizing Repetition, and Three Reads. Each routine targets a specific standard for mathematical practice, but they all share common design features that keep a laser focus on math thinking and provide access to a wide range of learners. A brief description of each reasoning routine and a visual that shows the repeatable flow of each routine is given in Figure 2–1. The icons within each visual highlight the designs for interaction—how students engage with each other, the content, and the teacher—that remain the same within each routine.

Capturing Quantities

1 Launch Routine

THINKING GOAL
Reasoning quantitatively

2 Identify Quantities & Relationships
Individual Think Time | Pairs | Share, Discuss, & Annotate

3 Create Diagrams
Individual Think Time | Pairs

4 Discuss Diagrams
Individual Think Time | Pairs | Share, Discuss, & Annotate

5 Reflect on Your Thinking
Individual Write Time | Pairs | Share & Record

The goal of the Capturing Quantities reasoning routine is to develop quantitative reasoning (Common Core State Standards [CCSS] Standards for Mathematical Practice [SMP] 2, Reason abstractly and quantitatively [National Governors Association Center for Best Practices, Council of Chief State School Officers 2010]). In the routine, students identify quantities and relationships in a problem situation, work with a partner to create a diagram that shows all the quantities and the relationships among them, then share diagrams in the full group and discuss where/how they see various quantities and relationships in the diagrams. Finally, students reflect on what they have learned about reasoning quantitatively.

Connecting Representations

1 Launch Routine

THINKING GOAL
Reasoning structurally

2 Make Connections
Individual Think Time | Pairs

3 Share and Study Connections
Partner Share | Share, Discuss, & Annotate

4 Create Representations
Individual Think Time | Pairs | Share, Discuss, & Annotate

5 Reflect on Your Thinking
Individual Write Time | Pairs | Share & Record

The goal of the Connecting Representations reasoning routine is to develop structural thinking (CCSS SMP 7, Look for and make use of structure). In the routine, students analyze and then work with a partner to connect two different types of representations, share and study connections in the full group, then create, share, and discuss a missing representation. Finally, students reflect on what they have learned about thinking structurally. You saw a glimpse of this routine in Mr. Ryan's class in Chapter 1.

Figure 2–1

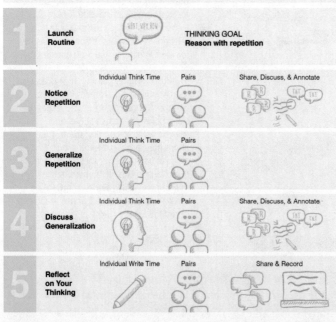

Recognizing Repetition

1 Launch Routine	WHAT, WHY, HOW	THINKING GOAL **Reason with repetition**
2 Notice Repetition	Individual Think Time / Pairs / Share, Discuss, & Annotate	
3 Generalize Repetition	Individual Think Time / Pairs	
4 Discuss Generalization	Individual Think Time / Pairs / Share, Discuss, & Annotate	
5 Reflect on Your Thinking	Individual Write Time / Pairs / Share & Record	

The goal of the Recognizing Repetition reasoning routine is to develop repeated reasoning (CCSS SMP 8, Look for and express regularity in repeated reasoning). In the routine, students engage in a counting, constructing, or calculating process and sense the regularity, share repetitions they are noticing, and then work with a partner to generalize the repetition. They then share and discuss generalizations in the full group, and finally, they reflect on what they have learned about reasoning through repetition.

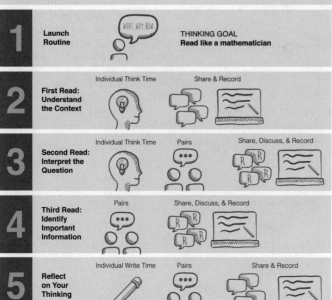

3 Reads

1 Launch Routine	WHAT, WHY, HOW	THINKING GOAL **Read like a mathematician**
2 First Read: Understand the Context	Individual Think Time / Share & Record	
3 Second Read: Interpret the Question	Individual Think Time / Pairs / Share, Discuss, & Record	
4 Third Read: Identify Important Information	Pairs / Share, Discuss, & Record	
5 Reflect on Your Thinking	Individual Write Time / Pairs / Share & Record	

The goal of the Three Reads reasoning routine is to make sense of math problems (CCSS SMP 1, Make sense of problems and persevere in solving them). In the routine, students read a word problem three times, each time for a different purpose. After the first read, students make sense of the context, answering, "What's the problem about?" After the second read, pairs restate the question in their own words, and share and discuss their rephrased questions. After the third read, students identify important information and as a group share and record information. Finally, students reflect on what they've learned about reading and interpreting a math problem.

Figure 2–1 (*continued*)

How Do Reasoning Routines Create a Math Thinking Learning Environment?

In Chapter 1 we said that thinking classrooms contain three key ingredients: they position students to think and reason mathematically, they provide time to think and reason, and they provide collaborative structures within which to think and reason. In this section we will explain how our reasoning routines create a math thinking learning environment.

Students Think and Reason Mathematically

Our reasoning routines are explicitly designed to develop mathematical thinking. Each routine is driven by a clearly articulated math thinking goal, makes use of ask-yourself questions and sentence frames and starters that prompt mathematical thinking, and ends with a meta-reflection so that students can name and solidify what they have learned about thinking like a mathematician.

Thinking Goal

Each routine for reasoning begins with the teacher clearly stating the type of thinking students will be developing as they engage in the routine. A thinking goal not only provides common language to talk about the mathematical thinking, it also communicates that the focus of the lesson is not the answer nor the steps taken, but rather sharing and explaining how students are making sense of the problem, what they think is mathematically important, the things they are paying attention to, and the questions they are asking themselves that are driving their problem solving. In short, the purpose of the lesson is to build a math thinking muscle. Some examples of thinking goals from the routines we just described include:

- Learn to identify quantities and relationships in problem situations (Capturing Quantities).
- Learn to connect numeric expressions to visuals (Connecting Representations).
- Learn to record and track repetition in your calculations (Recognizing Repetition).
- Learn to read a math problem three times to understand the context, to understand the question, and to identify important information (Three Reads).

Thinking Prompts

Two types of thinking prompts—ask-yourself questions and sentence starters and frames—are used throughout each reasoning routine to maintain focus on the thinking goal. Ask-yourself questions (e.g., "What are the important quantities in this situation?"

or "What would a mathematician think was important about this?") are posed to orient initial sense making of a math problem or representation. They shift the focus from "What should I do?" to "What would be helpful to consider?" Sentence frames and starters are used to ensure a focus on thinking when students begin talking with a partner or sharing in the full group. Rather than students starting with the answer they got and what they did, these prompts orient students to begin their conversations with what they are noticing or wondering (i.e., they begin with their thinking). We will talk more about both of these types of thinking prompts later in the chapter.

Meta-Reflection

Every reasoning routine ends with a meta-reflection in which students reflect on what they have learned about thinking like a mathematician. Sentence frames are provided to focus student reflections on the thinking (see Figure 2–2). After individual writing time, students discuss their reflections with a partner and the teacher listens in to select reflections to share and record in the full group. These recorded thinking takeaways become touchstones students can reference in future lessons.

- When looking for quantities in a word problem, I learned to _____.
- The next time I interpret a _____ I will look for _____.
- When looking for repetition, I learned to ask myself _____.

Figure 2–2

Students Have Time to Think and Reason Mathematically

Thinking takes time. Each reasoning routine centers on one high-demand task, giving students the time they need to make sense of and grapple with that problem, as well as the various ways their classmates are thinking about it. For example, in the Capturing Quantities routine, students identify the important quantities and relationships in a single word problem and represent them with a diagram. The teacher posts a range of diagrams and students analyze each one, identifying the quantities and relationships from the problem statement that are captured in the diagram as well as any implicit quantities or hidden relationships that can now be seen in the visual. In Recognizing Repetition, students engage in a counting, calculating, or constructing process and identify and generalize the regularity in their process, and then the class shares and discusses student generalizations and the underlying repetition.

Each routine is designed to build the habit of pausing to notice, interpret, and question before moving to problem solving. To push back against many students' instinct to grab some numbers and calculate, each reasoning routine shifts the focus away from answer-getting and toward making sense of a situation, problem, representation, and so on. For example, in Three Reads, students read a word problem three times, each time for a different purpose. The focus is on pausing and interpreting a math problem before jumping to solve it. Similarly, in Capturing Quantities, students first identify quantities and relationships in a problem situation before re-presenting them in a diagram.

Look at the infographics of the four reasoning routines in Figure 2–1 and you will see that the think-pair-share structure is used throughout the routines. Each time students are presented with a task, they get some individual think time to interpret the task before working with a partner. Additionally, students always have some private think time to make sense of a classmate's work before discussing with a partner and then in the full group. Any time a visual is introduced in a reasoning routine, be it student work under the document camera or a posted chart, students have individual think time to make sense of the image before working with a partner or answering a teacher question. Finally, whenever a teacher poses a question during discussions in the full group, there is always a pregnant pause for students to think before turning to a partner to discuss a response.

Students Think and Reason Mathematically Within Collaborative Structures

Although students have individual time to begin thinking throughout our reasoning routines, the bulk of the mathematical thinking and reasoning happens in student pairs. The purpose of individual think time in our routines is for students to ready themselves to work productively with a partner, not to come up with an answer that they check with their partner. The pair structure provides students a safe space to share initial noticings, ask and discuss questions, gain another perspective, and collaboratively work through mathematical ideas and language. Look at the infographics in Figure 2–1 and you will see that partner work is woven throughout each routine. Similarly, turn-and-talks during all full-group discussions in the routines provide processing space for ideas and language when students share and discuss each other's thinking. The teacher uses talk moves (more about those under "The Four Rs," on p. 33) to support collaborative sense making during full-group discussions as students are expected to listen to their classmates and explicitly prompted to revoice their ideas, adding more detail and increasingly precise language.

Now that you know what we mean by reasoning routines and how they are intentionally designed to provide time and collaborative structures in which to think and reason mathematically, we want to highlight five essential instructional strategies permeating our routines.

Five Essential Strategies

The five essential instructional strategies in our reasoning routines are:

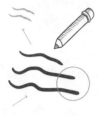  

I noticed...
so I knew...
so I looked for...
...connects to...
because...

- annotation
- ask-yourself questions
- Four Rs
- sentence starters and frames
- turn-and-talks.

We highlighted the first four essential strategies in *Routines for Reasoning* (Kelemanik, Lucenta, and Creighton 2016). Although we referenced turn-and-talks as a mainstay of language-rich classrooms and illustrated their use and impact in the vignettes of the routines, we did not explicitly label them as an essential strategy. We now include the turn-and-talk in our list of essential instructional strategies as we have seen time and again how a well-placed turn-and-talk during a full-group discussion can provide time and a safe, supportive structure in which students can work out their mathematical thinking and language. In addition, turn-and-talk is a very effective instructional strategy for stepping out of the middle and promoting collaborative sense making among students. In this way turn-and-talks are both a powerful student support and a strategy that teachers can leverage to develop a thinking classroom.

These five essential strategies promote the shifts in practice necessary for a thinking classroom—they maintain a focus on thinking, cause teachers to step out of the middle, and support productive struggle. Because these instructional strategies are baked into the design of our reasoning routines, the routines become effective vehicles for developing instructional practices critical for thinking classrooms.

In the next section, we will describe each essential strategy, how it keeps the focus on mathematical thinking, supports a range of learners, and helps teachers make the three critical shifts in practice necessary to teach mathematical thinking. We will also include instruction on how to get started with each strategy and highlight pitfalls to avoid.

Essential Strategy 1: Annotation

What Is Annotation?

Simply put, annotation is a visual representation of a student's verbalized mathematical thinking. During a full-group discussion, annotation can help students connect what they are hearing their classmates say to what they are seeing to make sense of a mathematical idea. For exam-

ple, back in Chapter 1 Mr. Ryan used annotation to highlight, as a student was sharing, where that student had noticed "three groups of the same thing" in the visual and algebraic expression they had connected. Mr. Ryan's annotation included purposeful use of color (red to show the number of groups and blue to highlight what is in each group in both representations), words ("3 groups of") and symbols (he drew a rectangle above the *x* and two squares above the 2, and placed an *x* inside the rectangle and a 2 on top of the squares in each row.) (See Figure 2–3.)

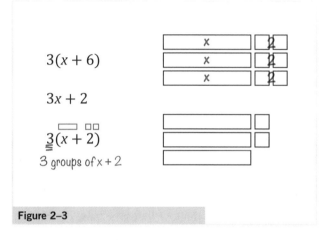

Figure 2–3

Annotation is not a one-time event; it unfolds as student thinking continues. In the case of Mr. Ryan's class, after the initial connection was made and annotated, he asked students to turn and talk about where they saw the parentheses in the first visual. As students shared and rephrased the idea that "the parentheses are like the rows," Mr. Ryan annotated the parentheses in red and then drew red parentheses around each row and added the numbers *1, 2,* and *3* to the rows (see Figure 2–4).

It is worth noting that we are talking here about annotation as an instructional move the teacher makes during full-

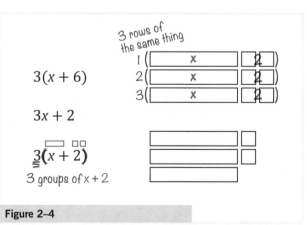

Figure 2–4

group discussions to keep the focus on the mathematical thinking and to provide support for students who struggle to access and attend to auditory input. However, annotation is also a tool that mathematicians use as they work with pen in hand to make sense of something and/or communicate their thinking to others. Therefore, in some of our routines, such as Decide and Defend (see Chapter 3), students are explicitly prompted to annotate when they are writing or drawing or presenting their written work in the full group.

How Does Annotation Keep the Focus on the Mathematical Thinking?

Annotation is neither scribing verbatim what a student is saying nor simply writing down what *you* want to show students. In reasoning routines, the teacher uses annotation to highlight the particular avenue of thinking a student is using when sharing in the full group. This is clear in how Mr. Ryan visually connected the three "chunks" or "three groups of the same thing" with his annotation of the connected visual and algebraic expression. In this way he highlighted chunking, an important aspect of structural thinking.

How Does Annotation Support a Range of Math Learners?

Annotation provides an additional processing modality by connecting the verbal to the visual—whether that visual is written or gestured. The visual component is crucial for English learners and students who struggle to process information auditorily. Annotation also provides focus for students who struggle to orient visually, and it also creates residue for students who lose focus, become distracted, or simply walk into the middle of a class discussion. In all these ways annotation is a powerful support to help students focus on and make sense of their classmates' mathematical thinking.

How Does Annotation Help Teachers Shift Their Practice?

As we mentioned previously, the goal of teacher annotation is to highlight and support the mathematical thinking students share and discuss during full-group conversations. This might mean labeling quantities students identify in a context, or circling friendly "chunks" of an irregular shape, or writing down how a student "changes the form" of a number in their head when they are doing mental math, or using color-coding to track the impact of an estimate in a mathematical model. In this way, the teacher is calling attention to the mathematical thinking in student explanations.

When teachers annotate, they step out of the middle and privilege student thinking. The teacher remains silent as they annotate, making space for students to share and discuss their ideas with one another in the full group. Thus, this role of annotator sends the tacit message to students that their ideas matter and are being discussed.

It is all too common for students to check out during full-group conversations when they don't hear or don't yet understand what their classmates are saying. Once a student checks out, it is very difficult for them to check back into the conversation. Pointing to the part of a visual or place in a solution strategy that is being discussed can help students reorient to what is being said. When the teacher annotates the image about which students are talking, it not only connects the words being said to a visual but also provides residue of the conversation that a struggling student can consider as the class discussion unfolds. This is a powerful support that can keep students, especially those who are strong visual–spatial processors, struggling productively.

Getting Started with Teacher Annotation

In this section we share some advice on how to prepare for annotating, along with when and how to annotate. In Chapter 6 we will provide activities and advice that will help you increase your capacity to annotate your students' mathematical thinking in the moment.

Preparing to Annotate

Although annotation requires being responsive to student utterances in the moment, you can and should prepare for annotating. Just like an actor rehearses their lines before the theatre fills or a sports team practices plays before the big game, teachers should work through annotation options before they are standing at the board in front of the class trying to highlight mathematical thinking that a student is sharing in the moment.

Following these steps when you are planning your annotation will prepare you well for doing it in real time:

1. Articulate your thinking goal. Are you focusing on quantitative, structural, or repeated thinking? Is there a particular slice of that thinking you are targeting? For example, if students are finding a calculation shortcut (as we'll see in Contemplate Then Calculate in Chapter 4), do you want them focusing on structural thinking in general or is the goal to target changing the form of a numeric expression to make calculation easier?

2. Anticipate how students might work on the task. For example, if your structural thinking focus is "changing the form" and students are asked to find a calculation shortcut to determine the value of $2 + 25 + 3 + 35 + 4 + 45$, what are all the ways they might change the form of the expression or the individual terms to make it easier to calculate?

3. Practice annotating. Reproduce the expression multiple times and practice annotating and reannotating the various approaches you anticipated so that the annotation highlights how the form of the numbers and expression is being changed. Consider how you might use color, words, symbols, visuals, and so on. Figure 2–5 shows some examples.

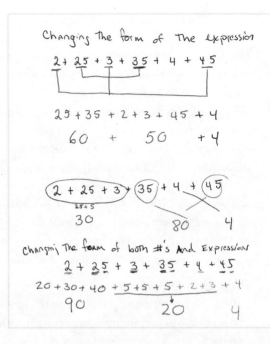

Figure 2–5

Planning for annotation is critical in that it will help you to maintain focus on your goal and better position you to hear the thinking in students' explanations and have some options for how to highlight that thinking. However, annotation is a responsive endeavor. It is crucial that in the moment you listen carefully to what your students are saying and annotate their thinking as it unfolds, instead of simply reproducing an annotation you prepared ahead of time. The goal of your annotation is to support your students as they make sense of and build on their classmates' mathematical thinking.

Implementing Annotating

In the classroom, the first step to annotating in the moment is listening carefully to what students are saying. That process begins before the class discussion as you tour the room listening in on partner conversations in advance of the full-group share. This allows you to get a sense of the thinking in the room and, ideally, select students to share particular lines of thought, as opposed to cold calling and not knowing what a student is going to say.

Annotation is most powerful when teachers allow an idea to percolate before annotating. So, during full-group discussions, we recommend that you do not make any annotations when a student idea is first shared. Feel free to point (or gesture) as the student initially shares their idea, then begin your annotation on the rephrase. We recommend waiting for a couple reasons. First, waiting to annotate on the rephrase provides every student in the class an opportunity to process what their classmate is saying. If you annotate as an idea is first being shared, you are in effect processing the idea, which robs the rest of the class of the opportunity to process what the students heard their classmate say. Pointing can help students track what is being talked about without processing it for them. Another reason to wait to annotate is that it gives you time to make sense of what the student said and think about how you can highlight the underlying mathematical thinking. When a student shares, listen for the mathematical thinking underlying their strategy. Listen for what it was they were noticing or knew that jump-started their approach. This prepares you to annotate more accurately and effectively during the rephrase. Do not feel as though you have to annotate everything on the first rephrase; you can (and should!) add more annotation as the discussion continues and the mathematical thinking unfolds.

Some practical suggestions follow:

- Use color, but not too many colors. Color is a powerful tool for highlighting connections. Using more than three colors will make the annotation too busy and cause visual noise. We try to stick with two easily distinguishable colors— red and blue.

- Use shading and symbols. If you do not have color (or even if you do!), lean on different types (dotted, solid, dashed) and thicknesses of lines as well as arrows, shapes, and grouping symbols, for example: { }, [ ], ( ).

- Include words, but not too many. Record any words or phrases that are critical to the discussion and thus would support students' participation in the discussion.

- Less is more. Start with a little annotation. You can always add more as the conversation continues.

Annotation Pitfalls

Following are three pitfalls that keep teacher annotation from being effective:

- Focusing on the answer. Annotation is meant to make mathematical thinking and reasoning visible. We make it a practice never to write down the answer, as we have found that as soon as we do, student attention shifts to what they got and if it is right, and the thinking and reasoning gets lost.

- Reproducing an annotation you practiced instead of annotating what a student is actually saying. Annotation helps students make sense of what their classmates are discussing, so if a student is saying one thing and you are annotating something different, it will only confuse students. And that can inadvertently send the message that the student ideas are inadequate or unimportant.

- Annotating after the student has stopped talking. If you find yourself continuing to annotate after the student has stopped speaking, in all likelihood you have moved beyond representing student thinking and are starting to show how you are thinking about the problem.

Essential Strategy 2: Ask-Yourself Questions

What Is an Ask-Yourself Question?

An ask-yourself question (AYQ) is a prompt designed to orient student thinking. AYQs are questions that productive math doers ask themselves to drive their mathematical sense making and problem solving.

Initially the teacher asks these questions, but the goal is for students to internalize them and deploy them on their own while doing mathematics. Following is a list of sample AYQs:

- What can I count or measure in this situation?
- How can I chunk this expression into pieces I can connect with a visual?
- How can I generalize the repetition in my counting?
- What do I notice that might be mathematically important?
- What assumptions does this model make?
- Does the answer make sense? Does the process make sense? Are the calculations correct?

How Do Ask-Yourself Questions Keep the Focus on the Mathematical Thinking?

AYQs are designed to target mathematical thinking and reasoning. They are meant to be asked when students are making sense of contexts; analyzing representations, models, and arguments; working to gain traction on a seemingly intractable problem or when they have hit a dead end in their problem solving and need to switch gears. Simply put, they are meant to jump-start and restart math thinking and reasoning.

How Do Ask-Yourself Questions Support a Range of Math Learners?

AYQs provide students a way to start thinking when they read a problem and get overwhelmed by all the words, or look at a complicated expression and shut down, or glaze over when presented with a new mathematical representation. For example, students who have internalized AYQs can jump-start their problem solving by reading a problem once and asking themselves, *What's this problem about?*; reading the problem a second time and asking, *What's the question I am trying to answer?*; then reading the problem a third time and asking, *What are the important quantities and relationships in this situation?* Rather than shutting down when being presented with a complicated expression, students can ask themselves, *Can I change the form of this to make it easier to work with?* When making sense of a new mathematical representation, the student might ask, *What might be mathematically important about this?* These are questions that start students reasoning mathematically, without telling them how to think or what to do.

How Do Ask-Yourself Questions Help Teachers Shift Their Practice?

AYQs are subtle yet powerful drivers of mathematical thinking and reasoning in the classroom. As we mentioned previously, they are designed to prompt a particular avenue of math thinking, not telegraph the application of a concept or suggest a procedure to use. In this way, they help shift student attention to focus on mathematical thinking.

When teachers pose an AYQ, they step out of the middle and position students to think and reason on their own and with each other. In those instances when student pairs or the entire class gets stuck and looks to the teacher for help, the teacher can pose an AYQ, pause to give students a bit of individual think time, and then prompt them to turn and talk through a response to the question, once again stepping out of the middle and setting up collaborative sense making.

AYQs support productive struggle because they combat learned helplessness. When a teacher poses an AYQ, they provide students with a constructive thinking prompt, but more importantly, by not telling students what to do, they send the critical message that the student is capable of thinking and reasoning mathematically. Over time, AYQs serve as an internal compass for students by starting their mathematical thinking and jump-starting it if they are stuck. They empower students to drive their own mathematical thinking rather than depend on an external source (often well-intentioned teachers) for step-by-step directions and to persevere through nonroutine problems.

Getting Started with Ask-Yourself Questions

Preparing to Use Ask-Yourself Questions

The first step in preparing to use an AYQ is to get clear on your math thinking goal or the kind of mathematical thinking students might bring to the task you are posing. Choose or craft an AYQ that will prompt that type of thinking. For example, if your sixth-grade students are working on a ratios unit and struggling to distinguish between part-part and part-whole relationships in word problems, then posing an AYQ like "Ask yourself, '*What are the important quantities in this situation?*'" can help reorient them when they get stuck.

If you are working within one of our reasoning routines, AYQs will already be built into that routine. To prepare, look over the routine and make note of the AYQ(s) and consider what responses to the question(s) might sound like.

If you are crafting your own AYQs, keep in mind that an effective AYQ has two qualities: it orients to and develops mathematical thinking and it is neither too vague (e.g., "What do I know?") nor problem-specific ("What do I know about 17 and 5?"). These two qualities make AYQs usable across a wide range of concepts and problem types. When crafting AYQs for a specific avenue of thinking or a reasoning routine we are developing, we often ask ourselves, *What would a mathematician ask?*, and check to make sure the question doesn't just apply to this particular problem but can be used in a broad range of problem-solving situations.

Implementing Ask-Yourself Questions

Specific AYQs are built into all our reasoning routines. They typically tee up individual think time when students begin exploring a math task or when students pause to interpret a representation or a classmate's work. However, AYQs are also terrific prompts for getting students unstuck or when you want to orient students to a particular avenue of thinking.

If you are posing an AYQ to jump-start student thinking, pose the question and provide individual think time before transitioning students to partner work, a turn-and-talk, or full-group discussion. If you are posing an AYQ to restart thinking when a student pair or small group is stuck, ask the question and then walk away to give students time and space to think.

When posing an AYQ, you are not only trying to *prompt student thinking*, you are *teaching an aspect of mathematical thinking* (i.e., the kinds of questions mathematicians ask themselves when grappling with a math problem). Therefore, you must be explicit. When implementing an AYQ:

1. Project or write in a visible place the AYQ you pose.
2. Model the language in the AYQ.
3. Provide some individual think time for students to consider their response.
4. Reference an AYQ when students are stuck.
5. Periodically have students reflect on questions they are now learning to ask themselves to start and jump-start their mathematical thinking.
6. Keep a list of AYQs where students can see it and refer to it.

Ask-Yourself Questions Pitfalls

Pitfalls to consider when implementing AYQs might include the following:

- posing an AYQ as a teacher question and not explicitly as a question that students should learn to ask themselves independently
- not giving students time and space to consider their response to the AYQ before transitioning them to partner, group, or full-class sharing

- closing an open-ended AYQ by adding follow-up questions that shift the focus to an answer or procedure rather than the student thinking.

Essential Strategy 3: The Four Rs: repeat, rephrase, reword, and record

What Are the Four Rs?

The Four Rs are discourse moves that engage students in each other's mathematical thinking—but only if it is the students who are doing the talking and thinking. The Four Rs are:

1. Repeat. Students repeat a classmate's thinking exactly how it was stated.
2. Rephrase. Students rephrase a classmate's thinking in their own words, perhaps adding more detail.
3. Reword. Students reword a line of thinking using more precise mathematical language.
4. Record. The teacher records words or phrases being used by the class during full-group discussions.

Taken together, the Four Rs help students process and develop mathematical ideas and language and refine both so that they can articulate their thinking with increased precision.

How Do the Four Rs Keep the Focus on the Math Thinking?

In a thinking classroom the focus of the Four Rs is always on mathematical thinking. Students repeat, rephrase, and reword their classmates' thinking, not their answers or calculations. In this way, we help surface, process, develop, and refine how a classmate has come to approach a problem the way they did—what they attended to or knew or asked themselves.

How Do the Four Rs Support a Range of Math Learners?

Have you ever talked to yourself while thinking through a complex task? We have! Like us, many learners process ideas out loud. The Four Rs create space for students to process a classmate's thinking by rephrasing their idea or rewording it with more precision. When classmates repeat, rephrase, and reword each other's thinking, English learners and students who struggle to process auditory information get multiple passes at hearing that idea. The Four Rs also provide English learners regular opportunities to speak in math class. Recording language that students can reference during class discussions increases students' participation and helps increase English learners' language production, as does asking English learners to repeat what they heard a classmate say or reword a mathematical idea using language the teacher just modeled.

How Do the Four Rs Help Teachers Shift Practice?

The target of the Four Rs is always mathematical thinking and reasoning. Revoicing and having the opportunity to hear a classmate's line of reasoning multiple times provides all students the opportunity to articulate, process, develop, and refine mathematical thinking. The support the Four Rs provides students to work with and work through their classmates' mathematical thinking cannot be overstated.

The Four Rs is also a powerful tool for a teacher who is working to step out of the middle. When a teacher shifts from being the one who is repeating, rephrasing, and rewording to having students be the revoicers, they quite literally step out of the middle and explicitly orient students to each other's ideas. Repeating what our students say can be a hard habit to break. Many of us have been doing it for years, and for good reason. We repeat student ideas because we want to make sure everyone heard them and because we want to make sure they are stated as clearly and completely as possible. But when we are the ones revoicing student ideas, we inadvertently send the message to our students that they don't have to listen to each other, and this flies in the face of a classroom in which students are co-constructors of their mathematical ideas.

The Four Rs provide students who are struggling to follow a class discussion multiple opportunities to process what they are hearing. Having a struggling student rephrase a classmate's mathematical idea keeps them engaged and thinking productively about that idea. This repetition is critical for students who are working to make sense of a complicated mathematical idea.

Getting Started with the Four Rs

Preparing to Use the Four Rs

Although many of the decisions teachers make regarding the Four Rs are made in the moment, it's important to consider beforehand how to use them to further the thinking goal. This is because when you hear a student idea that is related to the goal, you will want to pause and use one or more of the Four Rs to provide students the support and space to process and refine that math idea and language. Taking time before the lesson to anticipate how students might talk about and around the goal will better prepare you to connect student utterances to the goal in the moment.

Implementing the Four Rs

In our reasoning routines, the Four Rs are used during full-class discussions. We also see these discourse moves used by students during partner and small-group work once they become a habit in the classroom. When you are thinking about when to use which *R*, consider the following.

After a student shares their mathematical thinking:

- If you think not everyone heard the idea, then ask that student or another student to repeat the line of thinking.

- If you are confident everyone heard the idea and needs to process it, then ask one or two students to rephrase the line of thinking in their own words.

- If you are confident that everyone heard and understands the idea but think that students could (and should!) communicate it more precisely using specific mathematical language, then ask students to reword the line of thinking. This may require you to prompt, provide, and/or model particular mathematical words and phrases.

- If there is specific language being used to communicate the idea that would be helpful for students to reference, then record those words or phrases publicly.

The first step to implementing the Four Rs is to not talk, and then think about why you were going to say what you were going to say. Knowing why you were going to speak will help you know which *R* to prompt.

Following are steps to integrating the Four Rs in the mathematical discourse in your classroom:

1. Preview the Four Rs. Before asking a student to share their thinking, for example, tell students that after a student shares, you will ask another student to rephrase their classmate's thinking.

2. Provide a sentence frame orienting to the thinking (e.g., "They noticed _____ so they _____" or "When they saw _____ it made them think _____ because _____") for students to use when they rephrase their classmate's idea.

3. Remind students to use the sentence frame.

4. Monitor the rephrase and ensure it is in fact a revoicing of their classmate's statement and not, for example, an explanation of what their own strategy was.

Be patient with students (and yourself!). It is not unusual the first couple times you ask for a rephrase to have the student explain their own thinking instead. Acknowledge it and gently ask for a rephrase of the original classmate's idea before moving on to this new idea. If you think that your students may bristle and ask why they have to rephrase or why you are no longer repeating or rewording important ideas, take the time to explain and ask them to help you step out of the middle and privilege their mathematical thinking and reasoning.

Four Rs Pitfalls

Pitfalls to consider when implementing the Four Rs might include the following:

- allowing the discussion to shift if students begin to rephrase but then talk about their own thinking, rather than reorienting to the original idea

- falling into the trap of repeating or rephrasing student thinking, instead of prompting students to be the ones doing the revoicing

- focusing the Four Rs on procedures and steps taken instead of the underlying mathematical thinking.

I noticed...
so I knew...
so I looked for...
...connects to...
because...

Essential Strategy 4: Sentence Starters and Frames

What Are Sentence Starters and Frames?

A sentence starter or frame is a skeleton of a sentence that helps students organize and communicate their thinking. A sentence starter like "A question I learned to ask myself when interpreting a diagram is _____" orients student communication. A sentence frame like "When I saw _____ it made me think _____ so I _____" helps students organize their thinking to communicate it more clearly. Both starters and frames give students a running start in communicating their idea.

How Do Sentence Starters and Frames Keep the Focus on the Math Thinking?

All the sentence starters and frames in our reasoning routines prompt mathematical thinking. Rather than focusing on answers and steps (e.g., "I got _____ by _____"), they focus on the mathematical thinking that led to the steps and answers (e.g., "We noticed _____ so we _____"). Whether the object of the starter or frame is the student themselves ("I saw _____ so I connected _____") or a classmate ("They noticed _____ so they _____"), the goal is always to uncover and communicate mathematical thinking and reasoning.

Sentence frames and starters can also be used to help students develop thinking language. For example, if you are working on quantitative reasoning with students, sentence starters like "The number of _____" and "The amount of _____" can help them shift from talking about the numbers in a math problem (e.g., 24 and 12) to naming the quantities those numbers represent (e.g., "the number of cookies with chips and the number of cookies without chips"). Likewise, if you are developing structural thinking, using a sentence frame like "I changed the form of _____ to _____" provides language for students to talk about this aspect of structural thinking. Following are some more sample sentence starters and frames we find helpful:

- They represented _____ by _____.
- Every time they _____.
- I agree/disagree with your defense because _____.
- We noticed _____ so we _____.
- An assumption this model makes is _____.

How Do Sentence Starters and Frames
Support a Range of Math Learners?

For an English learner, starters and frames support language production and often provide the nudge they need to share their thinking in class. A sentence frame can help a student who struggles with executive functioning organize their thinking when they share orally in class. For students who struggle with anxiety, using a sentence starter or frame when turning to talk with a partner can mean the difference between speaking and not speaking. Although they are critical supports for some students, sentence starters and frames can help *all* students communicate their math thinking and reasoning.

How Do Sentence Starters and Frames Help Teachers Shift Practice?

All too often, when we ask students to share, they give their answer and say what they did, and omit how it was they came to do what they did (i.e., their mathematical thinking). Even when we explicitly ask students to "share their thinking," they almost always just tell us what they did. Sentence frames and starters push back against this instinct and force students to start at the beginning and share their initial sense making.

When we provide sentence starters and frames like "They noticed _____ so they _____" and "They represented _____ by _____," we step out of the middle and orient students to each other's thinking. These sentence frames send a clear message to students that it is their responsibility to be listening to their classmates' ideas and working to understand how they are thinking about the task at hand.

Sentence starters and frames support productive struggle by helping students to attend to, organize, and articulate their and their classmates' mathematical thinking and reasoning. When students share their approaches using sentence frames that prompt them to begin with what it was they noticed and how that led to their approach, the curtain is pulled back and what often feels like a mystery or a math trick to students begins to make sense (e.g., "Oh, you saw the multiplication and that made you think of area!"). When students are asked to rephrase a classmate's idea using a sentence frame that focuses on the thinking, they immediately begin to see why their classmate took that approach, and this will help them use that approach on a similar problem in the future.

Getting Started with Sentence Starters and Frames

Preparing to Use Sentence Starters and Frames

We use sentence frames and starters throughout all our reasoning routines whenever students are speaking to help them articulate their mathematical thinking and reasoning. If you are using a reasoning routine, look over these prompts and take note of the starters and frames used when pairs start talking, when students share in the full group, when students rephrase a classmate's idea, and when students reflect at the end of the routine.

If you are building sentence starters and frames into a lesson that doesn't use a reasoning routine, think about the type of thinking students might be using, then craft a sentence frame or starter that would help students articulate their thinking (i.e., what they noticed or wondered that drove their thinking). You will find that many of the starters and frames in our reasoning routines can be used in other lessons. We have found that they are the routine feature that students most readily transfer to other lessons. For example, after experiencing Contemplate Then Calculate (see Chapter 4) a couple of times, students naturally start with "I noticed _____" when sharing their thinking in other lessons.

Implementing Sentence Starters and Frames

We recommend using sentence starters and frames during these occasions:

- Students are sharing an idea.
- You want to orient students to a specific avenue of thinking.
- Students might need a starting point for discussion.
- Students are writing about their thinking.

It is critical that students don't see sentence starters and frames as optional or as a support for a subset of students. Although they are a critical support for some students, these prompts are intended to be used by all so that classroom discourse—be it in pairs, small groups, or the full class—focuses on mathematical thinking. Here are some steps to implementing sentence starters and frames in your lessons:

1. Project, record, or provide in writing the sentence frame or starter.
2. Model the sentence frame or starter.
3. Set the expectation that *all* students will use the frame or starter, because you want and expect all students to develop their mathematical thinking.
4. If students are sharing in the full group, remind them of the sentence frame or starter.
5. Hold students accountable for using the sentence frame or starter.

Sentence Starters and Frames Pitfalls

Pitfalls when using sentence frames and starters might include the following:

- using sentence frames and starters that do not prompt thinking
- providing sentence frames and starters for *some* students to use, not the entire class
- not holding students accountable for using them
- not listening carefully to how students use the frames and starters (for example, a student who says, "I noticed that I needed to multiply the two numbers and I got seventy-two" is not really saying what they noticed. They are beginning

with the sentence starter, but just saying what they did. In cases like this, ask the student to go back and say what it was that they noticed that caused them to multiply).

Essential Strategy 5: Turn-and-Talks

What Is a Turn-and-Talk?

Turn-and-talks are an opportunity for students to work out mathematical ideas and language with a partner. They differ from partner work in both scope and purpose. A turn-and-talk is relatively short (thirty seconds to three minutes) and is used to provide space to think out loud and gain an additional perspective. Partner work, on the other hand, is generally much longer (10–30 minutes) and is a structure for joint problem solving. Think of a turn-and-talk as a relatively short collaborative processing structure that provides every student the opportunity to speak and develop language and thinking. Because this processing is done out loud, turn-and-talks also allow the teacher to hear the range of thinking in the room, which is critical for selecting and sequencing student ideas.

How Do Turn-and-Talks Keep the Focus on the Math Thinking?

Turn-and-talks are used in reasoning routines during full-group discussions to provide students time and space to make sense of or drill down deeper into their classmate's thinking. These are not turn-and-tells, as in "Turn and tell your partner what you got for number 7." They are turn-and-talk about a particular line of reasoning (e.g., "Do you agree with their reasoning? Why or why not?" "What do you think they had to notice to use this strategy?" "Do you think this model is precise enough? Why or why not?"). We are fond of saying that if you give students a turn-and-talk, you have to give them something to talk about . . . a little mystery to figure out.

How Do Turn-and-Talks Support a Range of Math Learners?

Like the other essential strategies, turn-and-talks support a wide range of learning needs. For English learners, a turn-and-talk provides a safe structure in which to work out math ideas and work on the language to communicate those ideas, thereby increasing language production. For students whose strong suit is verbal processing, a turn-and-talk provides a space to talk through a mathematical idea. A turn-and-talk that is posed before sharing in the full group provides a hesitant speaker a safe place to work out an idea and practice articulating it. Building turn-and-talks into full-class discussions gives students who struggle to maintain focus times to stop and process what they are hearing.

How Do Turn-and-Talks Help Teachers Shift Practice?

Turn-and-talks can help teachers shift class discussions to focus on thinking, provided the prompt they have students talk about targets a mathematical line of reasoning or requires students to think.

A turn-and-talk literally forces the teacher to step out of the middle of a whole-class discussion and orients students to talk with a partner. During full-class discussions in a traditional classroom, the teacher asks one student a question, that student answers, then the teacher asks another question and another student answers, then the teacher asks a third question and a third (hopefully!) student answers, and the "discussion" continues along these lines. A turn-and-talk can be used to break this teacher-student-teacher-student-teacher-student dynamic that places the teacher at the center of the discussion. Instead of the teacher posing a question to the class and calling on a student to answer, the teacher poses the question and prompts a turn-and-talk so that every student in the room has an opportunity to consider the question and talk through a response with a partner.

Punctuating full-group discussions with turn-and-talks not only takes the teacher out of the middle and orients students to each other's ideas, but also provides critical processing time and space for students grappling to make sense of the task at hand. Regularly building turn-and-talks into full-class discussions can keep students who might tune out or give up engaged in the thinking.

Getting Started with Turn-and-Talks

Preparing to Use Turn-and-Talks

Preparing to use turn-and-talks is straightforward. Think about the questions you might pose when the class is sharing and discussing their ideas. Identify questions that will require students to think and reason versus telling an answer or simply recalling information. Consider crafting a sentence frame for students to use when they turn to talk with the partner.

Implementing Turn-and-Talks

Turn-and-Talks fall under two categories: those that teachers plan for ahead of time and those that they craft in the moment. Start by implementing planned turn-and-talks, and soon you will find yourself reaching for a turn-and-talk in the moment.

To get started, identify when in the lesson students will benefit from turning and talking. Then, craft a prompt to get them talking. When in the classroom, follow these steps:

1. Pose (and possibly record or project) a clear question or prompt.
2. Provide a sentence frame or starter to prompt partner talk.
3. Provide a time estimate (that you may adjust as you listen to students).

4. Listen to students as they discuss, and select and sequence responses.

5. Reconvene the class and remind students of the prompt.

6. Purposefully call on students to share their thinking and transition back to a full-group discussion.

Once you get comfortable with planned turn-and-talks, pay attention as student thinking develops and ask yourself when a turn-and-talk might be helpful to provide collaborative oral processing support. Here are four times we reach for a turn-and-talk:

1. When students need time and space to process a math idea and/or language before engaging in a full-group conversation, a turn-and-talk gives them that time and space.

2. When the teacher asks the class a question and no one raises their hand, a turn-and-talk provides the needed processing time.

3. When the teacher asks the class a question and all the students raise their hand, a turn-and-talk allows every student to answer.

4. When the teacher needs to hear how students are thinking to make an instructional decision, a turn-and-talk makes student thinking audible.

Turn-and-Talk Pitfalls

Pitfalls to using turn-and-talks effectively might include the following:

- Posing a vague turn-and-talk (e.g., "Turn and talk to your partner about what you heard"). Like a prompt that asks for information recall, a vague prompt is ineffective in prompting thinking and reasoning.

- Letting a turn-and-talk drag on too long. Typically, the room erupts when a turn-and-talk commences, and after a while the level of conversation begins to die down. This is the time to bring the group back together.

- Conferring with students during a turn-and-talk. The teacher's role during a turn-and-talk is to tour the room quickly, listening in on as many pair conversations as possible, so as to get a sense of the range of thinking in the room.

Chapter Summary

Although we laid out each of the five essential strategies individually, they are intended to be used together as a cohesive suite of supports in a thinking classroom. They work in tandem to keep the focus on the thinking, orient students to each other's ideas, and provide access and support so that all students are thinking and reasoning mathematically. Making these strategies a regular feature of your teaching practice will take time and attention, and the routines in this book can be great vehicles for this work. No matter which routine you begin with, you will find yourself posing AYQs to orient student thinking, annotating as students share their thinking, prompting students to repeat and rephrase their classmates' ideas, offering sentence starters and frames to focus and support communication, and using turn-and-talks to give students processing time and space. Over time, using these strategies becomes second nature in the routine, and you will find yourself migrating them into other lessons. We will talk more about mindfully building these practices and integrating them throughout all your teaching in the last chapter of the book.

The next two chapters introduce new reasoning routines. As you read about each routine, notice where the essential strategies are in the design. When reading the vignettes that show the routines in action, attend to how the teacher uses the strategies to get and keep all students working collaboratively to think and reason mathematically.

REFLECT ON YOUR READING

1. Reread the quote at the beginning of this chapter. What is one belief or practice you would like to alter to create a math thinking classroom?

2. How do reasoning routines promote mathematical thinking in all students?

3. Choose the essential strategy you would like to incorporate first in your teaching. Why did you choose that strategy? How might you implement it?

Decide and Defend

A Reasoning Routine to Support Constructing Arguments and Critiquing Reasoning

Ms. McKenna decided it was that time of year again—time to shift her attention to the dreaded state assessments. All year, she had asked students to find errors in worked examples and correct them. However, this was the first time she was asking her eighth graders to explain their thinking.

Ms. McKenna assigned the following task to students. Consider Nicole's work (in Figure 3–1). Decide if you agree with her work or disagree with it, and then defend your decision:

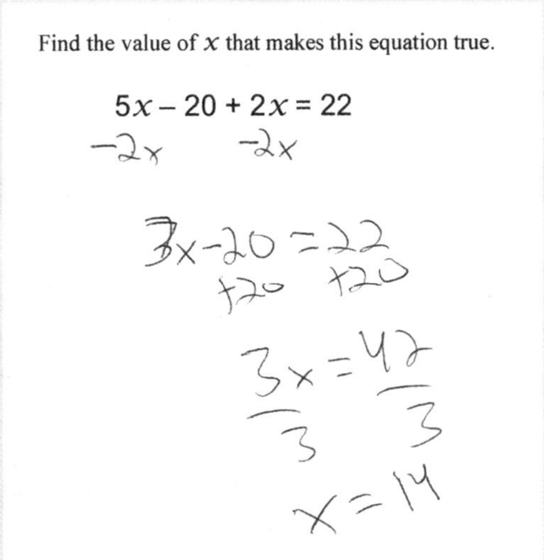

Find the value of x that makes this equation true.

$$5x - 20 + 2x = 22$$
$$-2x \qquad -2x$$

$$3x - 20 = 22$$
$$+20 \quad +20$$

$$\frac{3x}{3} = \frac{42}{3}$$

$$x = 14$$

Figure 3–1

When she sat down to analyze her students' written work, she saw a trend. Most students solved the problem on their own, determined the correct answer, and claimed that the original work was incorrect. Although Ms. McKenna was initially pleased that the majority of her students were able to solve the equation on their own correctly, she was frustrated that none of them began to dig into the student work and analyze the mathematics of the error. Claiming that mathematics is incorrect because you arrive at a different answer ("Nicole's answer is not right because when I solved it, I got $x = 6$") is hardly a mathematical argument. It does not provide mathematical justification. If students only compare answers, they don't have the opportunity to consider the mathematics that underlies the error. In this case, they miss the chance to highlight and articulate the meaning of equivalence when solving equations.

Ms. McKenna decided to engage students in the Decide and Defend reasoning routine with tasks related to big mathematical ideas in eighth grade to give students multiple experiences analyzing student work, deciding whether they agree with it, and crafting a mathematical defense of their decision. As a byproduct, students would also be preparing for the open response questions they'd see on the upcoming state assessment.

The Decide and Defend routine breaks down the process of constructing viable arguments and critiquing the reasoning of others (CCSS Standards for Mathematical Practice 3 [National Governors Association Center for Best Practices, Council of Chief State School Officers 2010]) and builds the habits of analyzing mathematical reasoning and creating mathematical justifications. Before we introduce and unpack Decide and Defend, let's take a look at what constructing viable arguments and critiquing the reasoning of others looks like.

What Does It Mean to "Construct and Critique"?

When we construct viable arguments, we attend to the mathematical idea at hand, potential lines of reasoning and their validity, and the representation and language we will use to communicate our thinking. We then ask ourselves questions to generate and articulate conjectures, assumptions, representations, and logical communication that become more precise with multiple drafts.

When we begin to critique someone else's reasoning, we first orient to an aspect of the work (the process, calculations, or results) to understand what is represented and communicated. Then, we ask ourselves questions as we consider the reasoning's validity and underlying assumptions, test examples and counterexamples, and continue to ask questions to clarify or improve the reasoning.

Figure 3–2 summarizes key questions we can ask ourselves and actions we can take when we construct viable arguments and critique the reasoning of others.

If you are constructing and critiquing, then you . . .

ATTEND to

Mathematical Concepts, Reasoning, and Communication

ASK Yourself

- What is the claim?

- Does the process make sense?

- Are the calculations correct?

- Is the result reasonable?

- Are the mathematical concepts valid for this line of reasoning and/or context?

- Is the argument sequential and complete?

- How does this representation support the reasoning (or communication of the reasoning)?

- Will another mathematical representation or concept uncover flaws in the reasoning or claim?

- Have all assumptions been clearly stated?

- Are there counterexamples and/or special cases that will uncover flaws in the reasoning?

- Is the level of precision in the representations, numbers, language, etc. appropriate and convincing?

- Are the mathematical concepts, language, representations, definitions, etc. understandable to the intended audience?

ACT

- Question thinking and underlying assumptions.

- Use and connect theorems, axioms, definitions, etc.

- Consider the impact of various mathematical representations.

- Communicate assumptions and constraints.

- Consider and use examples, counterexamples, and/or special cases to justify arguments.

- Adjust and refine arguments based on intended audience (relevant content, level of precision, representations, language, etc.).

Figure 3–2

In this routine, students analyze another student's strategy, a worked example, or a mathematical argument presented to them and then critique the reasoning that underlies it. In their response, they then justify their thinking by constructing their own argument. We will now dive more deeply into the thinking process and describe how mathematicians move through it. Since, in Decide and Defend, students engage in critiquing a worked example before constructing an argument, we will take a look at critiquing before constructing.

Critiquing the Reasoning of Others

When students critique someone else's reasoning, they draw on multiple sensemaking processes at the same time. They work to make sense of the mathematical content and consider its reasonableness. In addition, the approach or strategy often differs from one the students themselves would develop or create, resulting in a high-cognitive-demand process.

Consider the worked example in Figure 3–3. It is not a complete explanation of the student's approach, but it does capture their thinking. As you consider, reflect on what you pay attention to, the questions

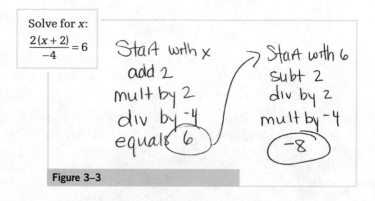

Solve for x:
$$\frac{2(x+2)}{-4} = 6$$

Start with x
add 2
mult by 2
div by -4
equals 6

Start with 6
subt 2
div by 2
mult by -4
-8

Figure 3–3

you ask yourself, and actions you take as you make sense of the student's reasoning. Take note of what changes in what you pay attention to, the questions you ask yourself, and the actions you take as you shift from making sense of the work to critiquing the reasoning.

You may have first oriented to the task and asked yourself what the question was asking. You may even have started to think about how you'd solve it yourself before looking to see how this student solved for x. Then, you likely read through the "Start with x" column and probably inferred that the student was "doing" the calculations as if they knew the value for x, and proceeded to read the "Start with 6" column and made sense of the "undoing" process. Regardless of the order, you had to wrap your head around the student's doing and undoing process before looking for accuracy or checking results. The process then continues by questioning whether the "doing" and "undoing" processes in the "Start with x" and "Start with 6" columns are accurate and in the correct order. At that point, you are probably beginning to decide whether you agree or disagree with the work and the thinking behind it—critiquing the reasoning.

As you critique the reasoning behind the work, you may ask yourself questions like, *Does the process make sense?* The doing and undoing process might resonate with you, so you take a closer look at the process to look at specific operations and numbers. You may have begun to question why the student chose to subtract 2 as their first step in the undoing process and looked back and forth between the two columns as you thought through their process. You may be tempted to start annotating the work, circling and drawing arrows to track and support your reasoning.

You might have approached the critiquing process very differently, starting by asking yourself if the answer was correct and evaluating the equation when $x = -8$. You would have convinced yourself the answer was wrong, and then dug further into the reasoning to justify your own thinking. What you pay attention to and the questions you ask yourself drive your critiquing processes.

Constructing Viable Arguments

As mathematicians construct viable arguments, they work through an iterative process in which they develop an increasingly clear rationale, make decisions about the kinds of representations and language that would best support their communication, and refine their argument so that it is complete and convincing. This process takes multiple drafts and layers of thinking, and therefore a good deal of time. For students, this process is succinctly captured as "Convince yourself, convince a friend, convince a skeptic."

Take a minute to draft a viable argument that makes the case that there is faulty reasoning in the student work in Figure 3–3. As educators, we are often in the position of correcting or pointing out how to fix student work. However, constructing an argument that is based in the underlying concepts is different.

To construct an argument, you may start by making a claim that states what you agree with and what you find problematic in the worked example. You may acknowledge the "doing process" as a means to "see" what is happening to x. That is, you may communicate that the student decompressed what is happening to x in the equation by listing the calculation steps in sequence. You may then justify the process of starting with the answer of 6 and reversing the calculations to discover a value for x. At some point, the argument must address the mathematical concept of "undoing" and the reversal of not just the operation, but also the order in which the operations are done. That is when you likely will consider the most powerful means of communication and ask yourself questions like, *What visual(s) will support my reasoning and help make it clear to a reader?* or *What additional language would help me communicate my argument?* Your draft argument may include color-coding, arrows to indicate process/order, conversational language like *undo* or *reverse* and mathematically precise language like *inverse operations*, or a context to provide an application of your mathematical reasoning, as in Figure 3–4. And, when this draft is complete, you may revise it to make your argument even clearer to its intended audience.

Solve for x:

$$\frac{2(x+2)}{-4} = 6$$

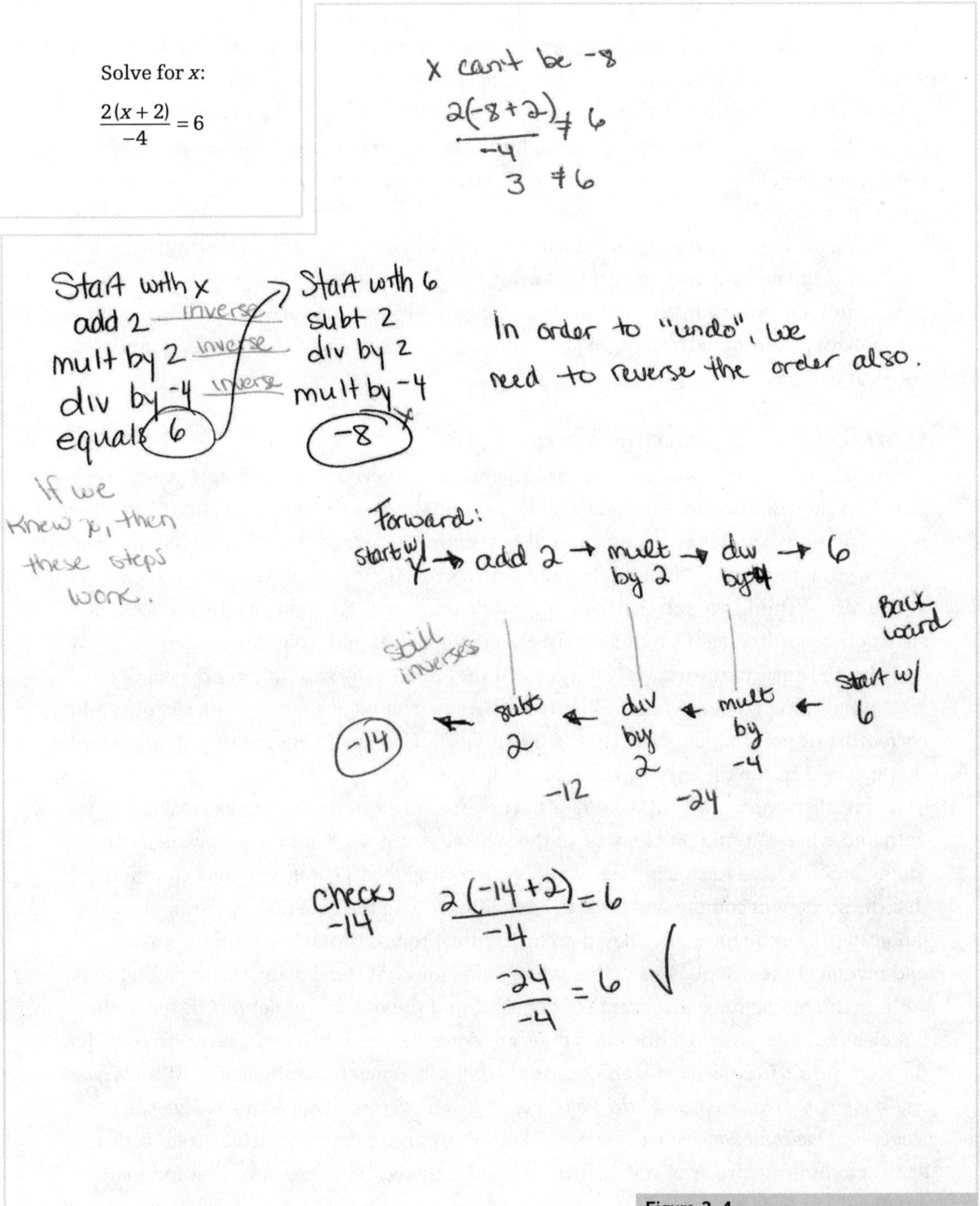

x can't be -8

$$\frac{2(-8+2)}{-4} \neq 6$$

$$3 \neq 6$$

Start with x
add 2 ——inverse——
mult by 2 ——inverse——
div by -4 ——inverse——
equals ⑥

Start with 6
subt 2
div by 2
mult by -4
⑧

In order to "undo", we need to reverse the order also.

If we knew x, then these steps work.

Forward:
start w/ x → add 2 → mult by 2 → div by 4 → 6

Backward

still inverses

⑭ ← subt 2 ← div by 2 ← mult by -4 ← start w/ 6

-12   -24

check -14

$$\frac{2(-14+2)}{-4} = 6$$

$$\frac{-24}{-4} = 6 \checkmark$$

Figure 3–4

Positioning Students to Critique the Reasoning of Others and Construct Viable Arguments

We often ask students to show their work using a mixture of pictures, numbers, words, or a process to "check" their answers. Although that might be good preparation for constructing viable arguments, it does not suffice. To construct an argument, students must first interpret a situation that positions them to make a claim; draft communication of their reasoning to support their claim; revise the argument, adding precision to both the mathematical concept and the communication of it; and adjust the communication based on their audience. A highly effective way to put students in this position is to have them make sense of someone else's thinking, decide if they agree or disagree with the thinking, and construct an argument to justify their decision.

An Overview of the Decide and Defend Reasoning Routine

In the Decide and Defend routine, students first make sense of another mathematician's worked example, then begin to decide if they agree or disagree with the thinking, and finally work together to create a defense of their decision. This routine builds students' capacity to analyze others' thinking as well as defend their own thinking. When students have multiple experiences in the routine, they develop an internal guide to interpreting worked examples and the means to justify their own thinking with increased sophistication and mathematical precision. Ultimately, students will transfer these habits of mind to work outside of the routine, and they will think and work as mathematicians whether they are answering an open response question on a standardized test or interpreting their own work in an attempt to increase its accuracy and/or improve the communication of their thinking.

The Steps of the Routine

Part 1: The Decide and Defend routine begins with an introduction to the routine, including the articulation of a thinking goal.

Part 2: Students then work to make sense of the worked example by orienting to the question the student who created the worked example was answering and asking themselves what the student found as an answer and what they did to get that answer. The class creates a common record of the steps of the work students are analyzing—the evidence they have found in the worked example.

Part 3: Students work with a partner to decide whether they agree with the work, or which aspects they agree with.

Part 4: Students then continue their work with a partner to draft a defense of their decision and together annotate the worked example to support their thinking.

Part 5: Then, in the full group, the teacher facilitates a discussion that digs into the mathematical content that causes dissent in the classroom and/or focuses on the various approaches that students have taken to defend their decisions.

Part 6: Finally, students solidify all the thinking that has been developed during the meta-reflection process, when they reflect on how they made and defended their decisions and how they might apply what they've learned in future problems.

Part 1: Launch the Routine

As teachers launch the routine, they communicate the thinking goal for the routine and review the steps. It is important that students understand that the goal is not to correct the worked example, but rather, to increase their capacity to make sense of another's thinking, connect the thinking to mathematical truths, and develop and communicate their own mathematical arguments.

Steps for Part 1

1. Display and explain the goal that shapes what students will learn and why they are learning it. For example, you might say, "Today we are going to think and work as mathematicians. We will interpret some mathematical work, decide if we agree or disagree with the thinking represented, and then draft and defend our decisions."

2. Project and articulate the flow of the routine. You might say something like, "We will start by looking at a worked example and figuring out what the mathematician did or found in the example, then we will continue to make sense of the thinking as you work with a partner to annotate the work to decide if you agree or disagree with the thinking behind it, and then draft defenses of your decision. We will analyze two or three of the defenses from the class, and end with a reflection to articulate what you learned about thinking and working as mathematicians today."

Part 2: Interpret

During the second part of the routine, students make sense of the problem at hand as well as the worked example. The focus of this section is strictly on the evidence that students see in the worked example. By the end of the Interpret phase, students will articulate a common description of the evidence they've identified.

Sometimes in the Interpret phase students may begin making decisions about whether they agree with the work. That's OK. This process is fluid, even though we try to break it down to make it more explicit for students within the routine. If you hear multiple pairs decide whether they agree or disagree with the work, it is an indicator that it is time to share their interpretations and transition to the Decide phase.

The timing of this part depends heavily on the complexity of the worked example. If the work is complicated and/or lengthy, students will need more time to sift through and articulate the thinking that led to the work. If the work on the page is minimal, students will need less time to state what they see and share it in the full group. Typically, this part takes between three and eight minutes. The complexity of the worked example in Figure 3–3 is midrange and may take four or five minutes to interpret, including individual think time, partner talk, and share-out.

Steps for Part 2

1. Orient students to the task that will be solved in the worked example if students have not yet seen it. Pose the AYQ "What is the question asking?" If students have already seen the task or one similar to it, steps 1 and 2 may be merged.

2. Allow individual think time. Project the worked example, and pose two additional AYQs to focus students' attention on the evidence in the worked example: "What did they do?" and "What did they find?"

3. Pair students. After providing individual think time, transition students to talk through their interpretation with a partner, using the sentence starter "I think they _____" and prompt "What do you think they did?"

4. Listen to partners describe the work they see and select one or two students to describe the work using sentence frames like, "First they _____, next they _____, finally they _____" or "They found _____ by _____."

5. Have students share. Call on students to share their descriptions using the sentence frames and record the steps they describe. This recording should be in a place (chart paper/whiteboard) where all students can see it and it can remain public to support students throughout the routine and in case you'd like to draw students' attention back to it later in the discussion.

Part 3: Decide

During the Decide part of the routine, students dive deeper into the worked example, first alone and then with a partner, to decide whether they agree with the thinking represented. Each student has a writing utensil (we suggest different colors) and annotates a shared copy of the worked example. At first, students work silently and parallel to each other, and then they transition to discussing their thinking and collaboratively annotating the work.

Steps for Part 3

1. Frame the decision-making process, including AYQs, and explain that students will work individually and then with a partner to annotate a shared copy of the worked example as they make their decisions. You might say something like, "Now you'll work to decide if you agree or disagree with the student work you've interpreted. I'm going to hand out a single copy of the worked example, and you'll have time to annotate it on your own and then collaborate with your partner. Who can remind us what annotation is?" (Students respond.) "During the individual think time, please use a different-color ink than your partner is using. Three questions to ask yourself as you make your decision are projected on the board and printed on the handout: 'Does the answer make sense?' 'Does the process make sense?' and 'Are the calculations correct?' Take two minutes of individual think time, and I'll let you know when to start your partner conversations."

2. During the individual annotation time, circulate to observe student thinking, and transition students to partner work by orienting them to the sentence frames "I think the work is correct/incorrect because _____" and "I'm not sure if the work is correct because _____."

3. Listen to student conversations and begin to informally assess the decisions students have made as you start to think about the direction of the full-group discussion, which will take place in Part 5, Defend Your Decision. Regardless of whether there is currently dissent or agreement in the room, you will want to begin to think about the approaches you might select and discuss. You'll have more time to listen and observe as students draft their defenses. You may see and hear students begin to defend their decisions if they agree with their partner or as a result of their attempts to convince each other. Again, this is OK; the process of critiquing mathematical thinking and defending the critique is more continuous in nature than the discrete steps of the routine. In fact, if you hear some defenses emerging, you'll know to prompt students to move to drafting their defense, and you'll have more insight into which defenses you might share in the full group.

Part 4: Draft Your Defense

Students now shift to consolidating and clarifying their thinking as they draft a defense to share in the full group. Provide them with the option to have a clean copy of the worked example (convenient to have on the back side of their first pass at annotating). During this time, they prepare what they will say and what they'll show to the class. The goal is certainly not for them to write an essay, paragraph, or even a complete sentence, but rather to capture the aspects of the worked example they may agree or disagree with and justification of their own thinking.

Steps for Part 4

1. Let students know that they will now move from making their decision to preparing a defense that they might share with the class. You might say, "Now you and your partner should decide if you'd like to work on a clean copy of the worked example. If so, please turn your handout over to the clean copy. Either way, you will now think about what you'd like to share with the class and how you'd like to represent it. You don't need to write sentences, but capture your thinking through your work and annotation. You'll have about five minutes to do this."

2. Circulate to observe and listen as students prepare their defenses. Make decisions about which defenses you'll share, whether you will ask students to share incorrect defenses, what mathematical ideas or aspects of argumentation each defense might raise, and the order in which you would like them shared. If every partnership has correctly agreed or disagreed with the worked example, then the focus for the class discussion will be completely on the kinds of arguments students make and characteristics of their defense. It is likely that students will need to come to consensus regarding the validity of the worked example at the beginning of the discussion, so you'll want to select varying student strategies to develop collective understanding and then shift the focus of the discussion to another approach or approaches to making the same case. In doing so, students have multiple passes to understand the content as well as the characteristics of viable arguments.

Part 5: Defend Your Decision

In the full group, preselected students share their defenses, and classmates work to interpret the argument and play the role of a skeptic. Students playing the skeptic role increase their capacity to critique another's reasoning while offering discussion points or adding precision to the defense that classmates share.

Steps for Part 5

1. Ensure students understand that as skeptics they will doubt what their classmates say, raise questions about ideas shared, look for holes or lack of evidence in arguments, and so on. It will likely be the case that students are "pretending" they have questions or find fault in an argument, but they are doing so to fulfill their role as a skeptic. You may only need to discuss this during the first few enactments.

2. Defenders make their annotated work visible to classmates. You may take a photo using your phone or laptop and insert it into slides, use software to capture the photo, place the work under a document camera, or have students recreate an aspect of it on the board or chart paper to discuss. Provide individual think time for students to look over the annotated work before listening to the defenders make their argument.

3. Frame the defender and skeptic roles. Provide sentence frames for the defenders to use, and preview the sentence frames the skeptics will use. You may say, "Defenders, you can decide who is going to speak, but please make sure you track what you're saying on the representation so we can follow it. Start with, 'We decided the work is correct/incorrect because _____' or 'We're still not sure about _____.' And, skeptics, your job will be to articulate the aspects of the defense you agree or disagree with or pose a question to the defenders. Remember that the question may be one that you really have or one that you think would be helpful for them to answer. You'll start with, 'I agree/disagree with your defense because _____' or 'A question I have is _____.'" Ensure that students can see the sentence frames throughout the discussion.

4. Facilitate the discussion as necessary and repeat with another student partnership or two if time allows and it makes sense to do so given the goal of the lesson.

Part 6: Meta-Reflection

As all our reasoning routines do, Decide and Defend ends with a meta-reflection. Students have the opportunity to articulate takeaways for themselves and hear from classmates so that they can apply the thinking they've developed the next time they construct viable arguments and/or critique the reasoning of others. If time is running short, it is better to discuss fewer defenses and save time for the reflection than to shortchange the reflection process.

Steps for Part 6

5. Allow individual write time. Remind students why they engaged in the routine (e.g., to build the mathematical habits of interpreting, deciding, and defending) and emphasize the importance of reflecting on their thinking. Explain that they will reflect by writing individually, sharing with a partner, and then sharing in the full group. Provide students with sentence starters and frames to focus their reflection (e.g., "Next time I interpret someone else's work, I will pay attention to _____," "Next time I interpret someone else's work, I will ask myself _____," "When convincing a skeptic, I learned to _____," "A new math idea I learned is _____").

6. Ask students to select one of the sentence starters/frames, and then write individually. As they write, circulate, but confer minimally; prompt a student to elaborate with details or examples, but do not engage in discussion about their meta-reflections. Begin to select reflections that highlight important elements of critiquing and constructing arguments that might be valuable for peers to hear.

7. Have students share their written reflections with their partners. Listen in as you continue to identify reflections that will be important to share in the full group.

8. Share and record. Prompt preselected students to share their reflection(s) with the whole class and record the reflections. This public record serves as residue in the classroom so that students may refer to it later and use it as an anchor chart for critiquing and constructing arguments.

Essential Strategies in the Routine

Each of the five essential strategies (annotation, AYQs, sentence frames and starters, the Four Rs, and turn and talk) are integrated in Decide and Defend (Figure 3–5). They all serve to develop students' capacity to construct viable arguments and critique the reasoning of others, but AYQs, the Four Rs, and turn-and-talks play central roles in developing and communicating student thinking.

Ask-Yourself Questions

AYQs support students' sense making during Parts 1 and 2 of Decide and Defend. Making sense of someone else's thinking can be particularly challenging for students, and the AYQs support this process and avoid students shutting down out of frustration. The AYQs in Part 1 ("What is the question they are answering?"; "What did they do?"; "What did they find?") scaffold the interpretation process and reduce the potential for students to be overwhelmed. As students begin to decide if they agree with the reasoning, they ask themselves, *Does the process make sense?* and *Does the answer make sense?* and *Are the calculations correct?* These questions scaffold students as they dig into the worked example and provide multiple pathways into the decision-making process. Over time, students learn to ask themselves such questions as they interpret mathematical reasoning—including their own!

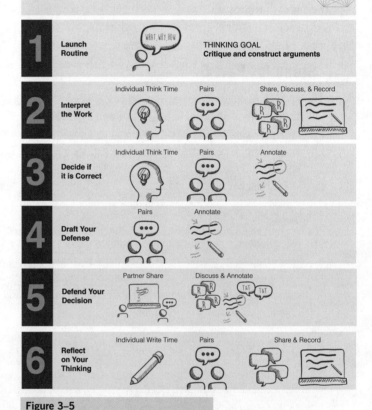

Figure 3–5

Four Rs

In the Decide and Defend routine, students share, analyze, and critique multiple lines of thinking, including the thinking represented in the worked example as well as the defenses shared in the full-group discussion. The Four Rs play a significant role to ensure that classmates hear, process, and refine the ideas. When students interpret the worked example, they name the evidence they find, classmates repeat or rephrase it to add clarity, reword to add precision as needed, and the teacher records it. Students are then able to refer to the written record and relevant language as they draft their defenses. As students share their defenses in response to the worked example, they may include a variety of representations and diverse arguments. Classmates need time and space to interpret and process them, and the Four Rs provide students with that critical processing opportunity. Students listen carefully as defenses are shared, knowing that they should be ready to repeat or rephrase the idea. Then, they hear the ideas multiple times and may even articulate them in their own words. The mathematical ideas and language become more precise with each pass, and student understanding of the ideas and language deepens—a win-win.

Turn-and-Talks

Turn-and-talks provide opportunities to draft and process ideas with a partner and develop accompanying language. Students sometimes have aha moments simply by saying their idea aloud to their partner. Together they revise or refine their thinking. Turn-and-talks also provide the teacher the opportunity to focus student attention on the mathematical concepts, mathematical reasoning, and communication in response to the discussion at hand and to gain valuable information by listening to how students are interpreting the worked example, whether they agree or disagree with the underlying reasoning, and how their defenses are developing.

Teachers prompt turn-and-talks as ideas develop in the full-group discussion to process mathematical concepts, representations, and/or the communication of the argument. In doing so, teachers can orient student attention to a certain aspect of a representation, classmates' defenses, or characteristics of effective arguments; provide students time to develop their thinking with a partner; and then build collective understanding when they return to the full-group discussion.

Although the essential strategies orient and support student thinking, they also provide teachers opportunities to put the three teaching shifts (focus on thinking, step out of the middle, and support productive struggle) into action. So, as you read the following vignette, pay attention to how the essential strategies play dual roles, supporting students and teachers.

Decide and Defend in Action

In this vignette, we will drop into Mr. Driscoll's seventh-grade class. Students in the class had worked on a surface area task (see Figure 3–6) the previous day, and Mr. Driscoll noticed a common error in their work. He mocked up a piece of student work to serve as the worked example at the center of Decide and Defend. Before reading further, take a moment to interpret the task and the worked example. Ask yourself, *What is the question asking? What did they do? What did they find?* Then, continue to decide if you agree with the work by asking yourself, *Does the process make sense? Does the answer make sense? Are the calculations correct?* Annotate the worked example as you make sense of it, to support your thinking and to lay the foundation for a defense of your decision.

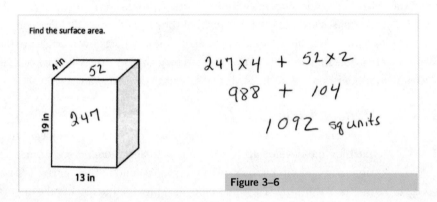

Figure 3–6

Mr. Driscoll's Seventh-Grade Math Class

Mr. Driscoll launches Decide and Defend by framing the thinking goal (to think and work as mathematicians, interpreting another's reasoning, deciding if we agree with it, and defending that decision) and reviewing the agenda. He then shares that students will be analyzing a worked example from one of the geometry tasks from the previous day. He orients students to the AYQs "What did they do?" and "What did they find?" and projects the worked example. Students have individual think time to interpret the work, and then they share their findings with a partner.

Mr. Driscoll listens carefully to how students are describing the work and selects Hugo and Daniella to share their thinking with the full group. As Daniella shares, Mr. Driscoll records for all students to see throughout the routine: *They found the surface area by calculating the area of one side and multiplying it by 4, calculating the area of another side and multiplying it by 2, then added it all together.*

Now, let's jump in at the beginning of Part 3 as students enter the decision-making process.

PART 3: DECIDE
Mr. Driscoll projects a slide to frame the decision-making process and asks students to recall what effective annotation might include (color, labels, arrows, language, and so on). He then previews the decision-making process.

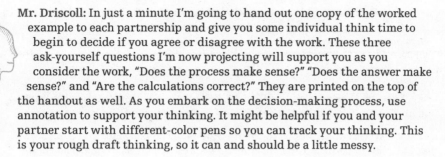

Mr. Driscoll: In just a minute I'm going to hand out one copy of the worked example to each partnership and give you some individual think time to begin to decide if you agree or disagree with the work. These three ask-yourself questions I'm now projecting will support you as you consider the work, "Does the process make sense?" "Does the answer make sense?" and "Are the calculations correct?" They are printed on the top of the handout as well. As you embark on the decision-making process, use annotation to support your thinking. It might be helpful if you and your partner start with different-color pens so you can track your thinking. This is your rough draft thinking, so it can and should be a little messy.

▶ *Mr. Driscoll makes the supports for productive struggle explicit to students. Students have access to the AYQs to guide them through the interpretation. In addition, annotation allows them to interact with the written work in a visual and tactile way.*

Mr. Driscoll observes how students are making sense of the worked example. Some students are carefully checking multiplication accuracy, some are redoing the problem on the side themselves, and some are circling calculations to draw attention to them. He notices that students have engaged enough with the worked example to begin discussing it with a partner, transitions them to partner work, and provides sentence frames to support their communication.

Mr. Driscoll: OK, I think y'all are ready to share the good thinking you've been doing. As you turn to work with your partner, start by stating your claim, "I think the work is correct/incorrect because _____," or articulate your confusion, "I'm not sure if the work is correct because _____." And, then, together, continue to annotate your shared copy to represent and support your thinking. I'm going to listen as you discuss, and I might even take a few pictures of your work.

I noticed... so I knew... so I looked for... ...connects to... because...

▶ *Mr. Driscoll sets clear expectations for how students will be working together, a precursor to stepping out of the middle.*

Mr. Driscoll circulates and listens to excerpts of partnerships' discussions.

....

Daniella: I think the work is incorrect because they have the wrong units on it. It should be square inches.

Hugo: I agree with you that it should be square inches, but let's check the calculations also.

....

Marco: I think the work is correct because I checked all the calculations and they are right. I also got 988, 104, and 1092 when I did the multiplication and addition. (*Puts check marks above 988, 104, and 1092*)

Vanessa: I think the work is incorrect because I don't think they should've multiplied 247 by 4. I think only 2 of the sides are 247.

Marco: Wait, what do you mean? Why would only 2 sides be 247?

....

> ▶ Notice that both Hugo and Vanessa made sense of their partner's idea, and took the next step to further their shared understanding. Both partnerships are engaged in the analysis process—evidence that Mr. Driscoll has stepped out of the middle.

....

May: I see why they multiplied 52 by 2, but I just don't understand this part where they multiplied by 4. (*Circles the 4 in 247 × 4*)

Michael: Well that's because there are 4 sides to the box after you count the bases. (*Tries to draw arrows to show all 4 sides*) It will be easier to see if we flatten the prism.

May: Oh, you mean a net drawing?

....

Carlos: I think the work is correct because each of the 4 sides has area 247 and the bases are each 52.

Brandon: OK, so how can we explain that? Is there a formula we can use?

Mr. Driscoll hasn't heard from every partnership, but he has observed enough to know that there is dissent in the room. He's happy about that; dissent always makes for a good discussion! However, he knows the discussion will first need to surface the error in the work, then uncover the conceptual understanding necessary to explain the error, and, if there is time, consider the ways in which students communicated their defenses. Mr. Driscoll continues to observe and consider which partnerships should share their thinking and in what order so that the discussion builds understanding of the underlying mathematical ideas and provides a variety of approaches for students' defenses.

> ▶ Notice that Mr. Driscoll intends to develop class understanding through the student thinking in the room. He doesn't plan to pull the class together and tell them why the worked example is incorrect. He plans to step out of the middle and orchestrate a discussion that allows students to co-construct understanding.

PART 4: DRAFT A DEFENSE

Mr. Driscoll is aware that some partnerships are ready to consolidate their thinking and draft a defense while some partnerships still don't agree if the work is correct or incorrect. He has confidence that, by the end of the drafting process and the discussion, all students will develop a deeper understanding of surface area and rectangular prisms. So, he pauses student conversations and asks them to draft a defense that they might be able to share in the full group.

Mr. Driscoll: Let's pull back together in three, two, one. Most of you have made your decisions and are ready to draft your defense. It's OK if you haven't; you can continue to ask yourself the three questions on the page to guide your thinking. When you've made your decision, some of you may want to start with a clean copy of the worked example, and some of you may want to continue on the copy you've both annotated already. The back side of your handout has a clean copy if you'd like one. In either case, it's time to prepare what you will show and what you will say. You don't need to write full paragraphs because you'll be supporting your annotated work with what you say about it. Then, we will take a look at a few defenses in the full group.

Mr. Driscoll continues to observe and takes pictures of students' work at various stages of their thinking. He decides to ask three partnerships to share their defenses for very different reasons. He has all three pieces of student work ready to project onto the whiteboard so he and students can annotate and record on the work. (Some teachers put the papers under a document camera.)

Mr. Driscoll wants to start by sharing Hugo and Daniella's defense (see Figure 3–7). They focused on calculations throughout their analysis. They checked the calculations in the worked example and recalculated the surface area on their own. They found a different answer and concluded that the work was incorrect. When Hugo and Daniella share their thinking, Mr. Driscoll will observe the class's reaction—some students may disagree still, believing the work to be correct. Based on that observation, Mr. Driscoll will decide how much discussion to have around this partnership's work.

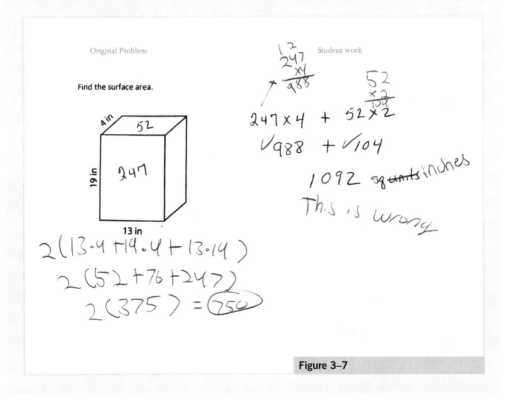

Figure 3–7

After the class analyzes Hugo and Daniella's work, Mr. Driscoll plans to have May and Michael share their defense (see Figure 3–8). May and Michael had a long conversation about how this net drawing won't fold back up into the original rectangular prism. This visual will help surface a justification for Hugo and Daniella's claim and might serve as an interesting approach to defend it.

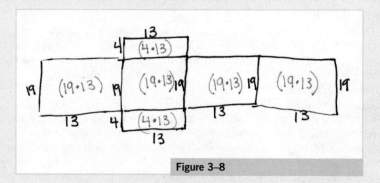

Figure 3–8

Mr. Driscoll plans to continue the class discussion by sharing Marco and Vanessa's argument (see Figure 3–9). They dig into the reason why the original worked example is incorrect. He thinks this defense will help students articulate the connection between the calculations and the rectangular prism. Ideally, he'd like for students to identify one of the underlying concepts—that an irregular rectangular prism has three pairs of same-size faces and/or the three-dimensional figure has "hidden" sides whose dimensions can be determined from the two-dimensional visual.

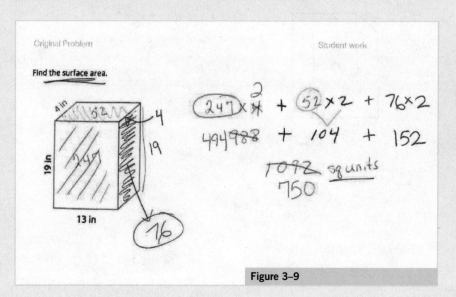

Figure 3–9

PART 5: DEFEND YOUR DECISION

Let's drop into the discussion of Marco and Vanessa's defense. The vignette picks up after the discussion of Hugo and Daniella's work and May and Michael's work. Mr. Driscoll has made the following observations throughout the discussion of the first two defenses:

- All the students in the class are convinced that the original worked example is incorrect.

- About three-quarters of the students can explain the error in rough draft language, using a lot of "that side" and "this length" to communicate.

- About half the class had an aha moment when students analyzed May and Michael's visual. Through repeating, rephrasing, and rewording, students came to understand that if all four faces were congruent, then the net drawing wouldn't fold back up into a rectangular prism.

Mr. Driscoll estimates that the class can spend about 6–8 minutes analyzing Marco and Vanessa's defense before transitioning to the meta-reflection. He decides to focus solely on students' capacity to describe the "hidden" sides of the three-dimensional figure and how they can use what they know to determine the measurements. He also knows that Marco and Vanessa's defense will give other students ideas about using color to support their communication of their thinking.

Mr. Driscoll: Now that we have looked at two different defenses that disagree with the thinking in the worked example, let's take a look at Marco and Vanessa's defense. Take about sixty seconds to make sense of their defense.

I noticed...
so I knew...
so I looked for...
...connects to...
because...

Marco and Vanessa, could you share your thinking starting with the sentence frames on the board, "We decided the work is correct/incorrect because _____. We're still not sure about _____." And, as you listen to Marco and Vanessa, remember that you are in the role of skeptics. As you all said earlier in our discussion, that means that you are "slow to be convinced." You might even ask questions that you actually already know the answer to.

Vanessa: We decided the work is incorrect because we, just like Hugo and Daniella, found a different answer. We tried to visualize all 6 sides and it was hard. Maybe we should've done what May and Michael did. Instead, we used color to show the sides that were the same size. There are 3 different-size faces, so we used 3 colors. (*Marco points to the three colors on the rectangular prism and the three colors in their calculations.*)

Vanessa: So, the red face on the front has a matching face, kind of like the back of a cereal box. The blue face is on each side, and the green face is on the top and bottom. (*Marco points as Vanessa describes where each color appears.*) The problem with the worked example is that they multiplied the red face by 4 when there are only 2 of them.

Mr. Driscoll: Can I pause you there, Vanessa? Who can rephrase what Marco and Vanessa have shared?

Andrea: They see 3 pairs of rectangles on the shape—a red pair, a blue pair, and a green pair. And, the original person saw 4 red rectangles somehow.

Brandon: Can I add on?

Mr. Driscoll: Of course, and Marco, can you continue to point as Brandon adds on to the discussion?

Brandon: It looks like Marco and Vanessa found two sides that the original work didn't have—the blue sides.

Mr. Driscoll: Aah. That's interesting. I'd like you all to consider those blue sides. How do you know their dimensions? (*Mr. Driscoll pauses to give individuals a few seconds to consider his prompt.*) Take a minute to turn and talk to your partner and together describe how you know the dimensions of the blue sides.

Mr. Driscoll listens as partners work to articulate how they know the dimensions of the two sides. He hears one partnership, Lee and Priya, refer back to the original figure and how they could label each side length with its correct dimension. He thinks that their description will help concretize the missing side lengths, and prompts them to share when they return to the full group.

As the discussion continues, Mr. Driscoll records language students are using and dimensions they are naming. By the end of the discussion, an organic word bank has developed on the board that includes: *faces, bases, side length, congruent, rectangular prism*. By the end of the discussion, Lee, Priya, and Mr. Driscoll have annotated and recorded on Marco and Vanessa's work as shown in Figure 3–10.

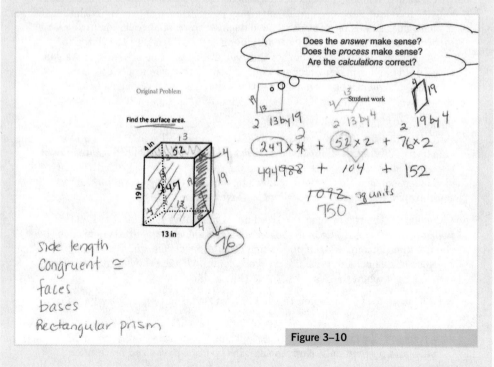

Figure 3–10

I noticed...
so I knew...
so I looked for...
...connects to...
because...

PART 6: META-REFLECTION

In the final step of Decide and Defend, students reflect on the thinking they've developed by completing a write-pair-share.

Mr. Driscoll frames the meta-reflection, refers to the goal of the lesson, and tells students to select one of the prompts provided.

- Next time I interpret someone else's work, I will _____ (ask myself, pay attention to _____).
- To convince a skeptic, it's important to _____.
- A new math idea I learned is _____.

He prompts students to write individually and begins observing student responses. Once he sees that most students have completed their reflection, he prompts them to share with their partners. As students do so, Mr. Driscoll listens in. He pulls the class back together and prompts three students to share their meta-reflections while he records them publicly.

Mr. Driscoll: Elsa, could you share your reflection?

Elsa: Yeah. Next time I interpret someone else's work, I will pay attention to sides I can't see and try to use dimensions I know to label them.

Mr. Driscoll (*as he finishes recording Elsa's reflection*): And, Hugo, can you share yours?

Hugo: To convince a skeptic, it's important to connect the drawing to the calculations, and color is helpful to do that.

Mr. Driscoll: Brandon, can you finish off our reflections for today?

Brandon: A new math idea I learned today is that you can color-code the formula for surface area to see where each piece of the formula is in the shape.

▶ *Mr. Driscoll selected these reflections because they focus on two important aspects of the discussion: using dimensions you know to uncover dimensions that are hidden and connecting a visual representation to related calculations.*

The Teacher's Role

Throughout Decide and Defend, teachers have the opportunity to enact the three shifts: focus on thinking, step out of the middle, and support productive struggle. In this example, the shifts may not always have been obvious, but they were critical.

Focus on Thinking

Mr. Driscoll decided to engage students in this particular task because of common errors he observed. He could have responded to the errors by showing students a correct example and having them correct their own work. Instead, he focused on the underlying concepts necessary to understand the two-dimensional representation of a three-dimensional object.

Throughout the discussion, he used students' thinking and their work to surface and highlight important mathematical concepts as well as strategies to communicate them.

Step Out of the Middle

Mr. Driscoll served as a facilitator of student thinking. He observed, listened, and made decisions about how to focus the full-group discussion so that all students advanced their mathematical thinking. He avoided kneeling down next to a partnership and engaging in conversation with them. When Vanessa made a pivotal claim, "The problem with the worked example is that they multiplied the red face by 4 when there are only 2 of them," Mr. Driscoll didn't get excited and say, "Yes, that's it! Those 4 faces aren't congruent!" Instead, students developed understanding of the idea through discourse—the Four Rs and an ensuing turn-and-talk. Students did the thinking and reaped the rewards.

Support Productive Struggle

The design of Decide and Defend provides ample time and supports for students' productive struggle. Students work through their doubts as they decide if the worked example is correct or not, consider why the worked example is correct or incorrect, and work to justify their defense. Throughout the process, students have the opportunity to question and revise their thinking, scaffolded by collaboration, annotation, and language supports. Although it might not have been visible to students, Mr. Driscoll supported their productive struggle in the way he selected and sequenced the student defenses. Each defense served a goal in the process: to establish that the worked example was flawed, to consider the underlying reasons, and to justify the defense through a variety of visuals and lines of reasoning.

Planning and Implementing Decide and Defend

Successful implementation of Decide and Defend requires careful consideration regarding mathematical content and student thinking, as well as particular preparation, to respond to students' ideas as they engage in the routine.

Getting Started

Choosing Tasks

Making sense of another student's worked example is cognitively demanding for students by itself, and then we ask students to draft a defense of their decision. As a result, this routine uncovers a whole lot of student thinking and lines of reasoning that create powerful fodder for class discussions. We strongly recommend starting with a worked example (correct or incorrect) that draws on previously learned and understood mathematical concepts. Selecting a common error is a perfect starting point.

The worked examples throughout this chapter all work well in Decide and Defend. Twitter is also a great place to find tasks, as many teachers around the country are developing their own (look for the hashtag #DeciDefend). To find or create your own, look through your own textbook, teaching materials, and standardized tests. Curriculum programs and assessments increasingly incorporate worked examples. Of course, your own students will probably produce the best inspiration for worked examples. Whatever task you choose, it should position your students to make sense of a line of reasoning that is not their own, and decide for themselves if it is correct or incorrect.

When selecting worked examples for Decide and Defend, ask yourself:

- Does the worked example highlight a common error students make?
- Does the worked example draw attention to a classic misconception students hold?
- Does the worked example contain a representation that will serve to deepen students' conceptual understanding?
- Does the worked example present a unique solution strategy that sparks consideration of underlying math concepts?

If the answer to any of these three questions is yes, then the task is likely a good one.

Introducing the Routine

When first using Decide and Defend, focus on establishing the predictable nature of the routine. We suggest having the same group of students experience the routine five times over the course of 1–2 weeks.

Some teachers choose to straddle the routine over two days to select and sequence student defenses without students in front of them. If you choose to do this, make sure you get through all parts of the routine so that you are establishing the experiences and interactions that remain the same each time. Doing so will ensure that your students and you internalize the routine's flow and purpose. Once the routine is established, use it whenever it makes sense, and the familiarity will be a support for you and for students.

Decide and Defend is applicable to a wide range of content. We find it particularly helpful as a means to reengage students in previously learned content in the beginning of the year or to prepare for standardized tests as the year progresses.

Preparing for the Routine

Because the flow of Decide and Defend stays the same each time, preparing to implement the routine allows teachers to dive deeply into the mathematical ideas that underlie the worked example and the kinds of defenses students may develop. The planning process involves being clear about the thinking goal and anticipating student thinking about the mathematical ideas as well as the ways in which they will interpret the worked example and defend their thinking.

1. Articulate the math thinking goal. To start, the math thinking goal will be general, such as "to build the mathematical habits of interpreting, deciding, and defending." As students become acquainted with the routine and the mathematical habits, you can provide more specific thinking goals (e.g., "Interpret alternate solution strategies" or "Use multiple representations to convince a skeptic").

2. Spend time analyzing the worked example. It's likely that you developed or selected it for a specific purpose, but you should also pay attention to additional mathematical understandings that the task may call upon. How would you interpret it? Do you agree or disagree with it? For what reasons? And how would you communicate your reasoning?

3. Anticipate student thinking. Have students seen the math task at the center of the worked example? If not, how will they make sense of it? How will students interpret the worked example? How will they describe what is happening in it? It will be helpful to anticipate their responses to "First they _____, next they _____, then _____" and "They found _____ by _____." This anticipation will support you as you listen to students and elicit and record their thinking. Will students agree or disagree with the worked example? What might cause challenges for students as they make their decisions? How might they draft their defenses—what language, representations, and lines of reasoning might they explore? If they draft the defenses you've anticipated, how will you orchestrate the discussion? Think about what student meta-reflections might be; anticipating exemplary student reflections will help you make decisions when facilitating the discussion.

4. Walk through the presentation slides (available on fosteringmathpractices.com) and insert the goal you've crafted and the task you've selected. Projecting a similar slide deck each time supports routineness and provides a visual representation of the cues and prompts throughout the routine. Devise a plan for sharing student defenses (document camera, taking photos, and so on).

5. Tweak the language of the directions, sentence frames and starters, and meta-reflections based on your task and your goal. Most of them will not even need tweaking!

6. Create two handouts for students. The first should have the worked example as well as the AYQs "Does the answer make sense?," "Does the process make sense?," "Are the calculations correct?" and plenty of space for student thinking and annotation. You will want extra copies of this handout so that students have access to a clean copy when they draft their defense (or put a clean copy on the back of the page). You will also need to prepare a handout with meta-reflection prompts for students to complete their reflections.

Resources including tasks, presentation slides, and a planning document can be found on fosteringmathpractices.com.

Decisions in the Moment

Throughout Decide and Defend, teachers serve as facilitators of student thinking. They step out of the middle and keep a dual focus on the underlying mathematical concepts and the lines of reasoning in students' defenses. As they do so, they make key decisions as they surface student thinking and process it in relation to the goal of the lesson. They need to listen carefully to as many student partnerships as possible and decide whether they need to clarify mathematical ideas during the full-group discussion, focus solely on the lines of reasoning in the defenses, or some combination of the two. Fortunately, in Decide and Defend, teachers have a few opportunities to circulate and listen and a good amount of time to make their decisions. Even still, there are many ideas to process and think deeply about. Here are a few tips and AYQs to guide the decision-making processes.

Taking in Student Ideas

There are three critical times that you will need to take in student ideas: when students interpret the worked example, as they agree or disagree with it, and when they draft their defenses. There is not a lot of time to take in the interpretation, so you'll want to position yourself in the room so that you can listen in on and see as many partnerships as possible. When students work together to decide whether they agree or disagree with the worked example, you'll hear their discussion and see their annotation. Finally, when students draft their defenses, they create written residue that is very helpful as you observe and take in students' lines of reasoning, and you'll have time to take in nearly every partnership's thinking. In addition, you can take photos of student defenses in progress to support you when you begin to select and sequence the defenses.

Selecting and Sequencing Student Ideas

As students decide whether they agree with the work, you'll be considering the dual focus of the full-group discussion. If a good number of students are struggling with the decision or making an incorrect one, you will want to start the discussion by focusing on mathematical ideas. If students are correctly agreeing/disagreeing, then you'll want to look at their defenses and identify their approaches.

Students' draft annotations are helpful supports as you listen and observe their work. Consider their line of reasoning. Are they using a counterexample, another representation, connecting representations, and so on to develop their defense? Is there an aspect of the defense that would be helpful for other students to interpret and be skeptical about? You'll want to make multiple passes through the room to see how thinking is developing over time, but it always helps to take photos as the defenses develop. You may choose to use an earlier version of students' defenses in the full-group discussion.

Analyzing Student Defenses

While facilitating the full-group discussion, teachers mine one or two defense strategies for deeper analysis through a turn-and-talk. You'll want to be clear about the focus of the turn-and-talk. Is it to deepen understanding of a concept or to highlight an aspect of a productive mathematical argument? Common turn-and-talk prompts focus on justification of a claim made in the defense and/or characteristics of the defense that are convincing. If the students in the skeptic role aren't asking questions, providing an opportunity for them to turn and talk to develop comments and questions will allow you to listen into their thinking and advance the full-group discussion when you pull back together.

Common Pitfalls

There are four pitfalls teachers often encounter (and we have too) when they first start using Decide and Defend. They include the following:

- misgauging the task
- focusing discussion on revising the worked example
- focusing on the completeness of a strategy or defense
- stepping into the skeptic role.

Misgauging the Task

Unfortunately, we know this pitfall well from our own experiences while developing this routine. We started by using a worked example that involved deep understanding of proportional relationships. Students could've solved the problem at the center of the worked example, but probably would've struggled to justify their strategies. And we asked them to interpret someone else's work on the task. It didn't go well; we got stuck in the interpretation phase. We scaled back the content of the task to a problem that we knew students could solve on their own and justify their own thinking, and students were able to engage in the complete process. So, we can't say enough: start this routine with content review to focus on students' capacity to critique another's reasoning and construct a viable argument.

Focusing Discussion on Revising the Worked Example

Students may start out by "fixing" or adding to the worked example to improve it. You'll know that's the case if you hear them saying, "If they just multiplied by 2 here instead and then . . ." or "I see what they did, but there's a better way to. . . ." That is a good starting point as they shift from their deciding phase to their defending phase. However, students also need to uncover the mathematical reasoning that lies beneath the worked example. Student defenses should focus on the validity of the reasoning rather than how to "complete" the worked example better. The full-group discussion should target and highlight the underlying mathematical concepts and the communication of them.

Focusing on the Completeness of an Argument/Defense

It is all too easy for the class discussion to shift to critiquing the completeness of a defense that is shared in the full group. If skeptics in the class start suggesting that the original partnership should add a label, include details of calculations, add language, revise penmanship, and so on, then remind students that we are looking at *draft* defenses. The conversation should focus on the thinking behind the defense, whether that is the conceptual understanding of the content or the types of arguments applied. Sometimes, the class looks at a part of a defense or an earlier draft, so this norm is important to establish.

Stepping into the Skeptic Role

We, as educators, have lots of experience playing the skeptic role. And it is easy for us to step in and ask questions that get to the heart of student defenses. However, that robs students of doing it themselves. Ultimately, we want them to be skeptics of work they interpret outside of the routine and of their own work, so the skeptic role is an important aspect of the routine and an important one for students to develop over time.

Frequently Asked Questions

How much time does Decide and Defend take?

As you embark on Decide and Defend, allow 40–50 minutes to start. In fact, you may want to do Parts 1–4 of the routine one day and Parts 5 and 6 the next day. This will allow you additional time to observe and consider student work. As you become more purposeful and clear with tasks and decisions, and students grow more facile with the routine, you may get it down to thirty minutes. But then, when exciting ideas emerge, you and students both will have stamina to discuss them, and you'll be back up to forty minutes as time allows!

Would you ever share a defense that isn't correct? (Students agree with an incorrect worked example, disagree with a correct worked example, agree for the wrong reason, and so on.)

Absolutely! In fact, sharing student defenses that will cause disequilibrium in the classroom is always a good idea. However, it is critical that you establish a culture conducive to this sharing ahead of time. Ensure that students use the sentence frames so that the discussion is about the work and the thinking, not the students themselves—the ideas, not the authors. To further position students to respectfully analyze an incorrect defense, it is helpful to pose a turn-and-talk that prompts students to identify an aspect of the defense they agree with or to develop a question about the defense.

Where does Decide and Defend fit into my curriculum?

Anywhere. Every math concept has common errors or misconceptions that can be situated at the center of this routine. Teachers choose to engage students in Decide and Defend at the beginning or middle of a unit to gather formative assessment, revisit prerequisite concepts, or introduce a strategy or representation. Decide and Defend is also helpful to solidify content at the end of a unit, because it surfaces and connects various conceptual ideas. Decide and Defend builds students' mathematical communication skills, perseverance in a big chunky problem, and capacity to interpret worked examples, all of which develop students' thinking and also help them prepare for standardized tests.

REFLECT ON YOUR READING

1. Why is it important to develop all students' capacity to construct viable arguments and critique the reasoning of others?

2. What about Decide and Defend and its embedded designs for interaction support students with learning disabilities? English learners?

3. What might be the impact on students' thinking if they engage in Decide and Defend over time?

4. In Mr. Driscoll's vignette, what moment stood out to you as being critical to engaging all students in mathematical thinking? Why and how was it critical?

5. What critical instruction shift (focus on thinking, step out of the middle, support productive struggle) will you focus on when you start facilitating Decide and Defend?

6. Which essential strategy (annotation, AYQs, Four Rs, sentence frames and starters, turn-and-talks) will you work to develop as you begin facilitating Decide and Defend?

Contemplate Then Calculate

A Reasoning Routine to Support Structural Thinking

As formative assessment at the beginning of the year, Ms. Swanda posted a Do Now problem for her seventh-grade students to work on and review some content from sixth grade. After observing many errors in student responses, including errors involving the distributive property, negative signs, and fractions, Ms. Swanda decided to discuss the problem as a class.

$$-3\left(x - \tfrac{1}{4}\right) = -12$$

To start the discussion, Ms. Swanda elicited values for x from her students. She heard a range of responses, none of which were correct, and recorded them on the board: $\frac{49}{12}$, $\frac{45}{12}$, and 4. She then asked students to find a partner who had a different answer and discuss the steps they took to solve the problem. She thought that comparing the procedures would help students uncover their calculation errors. As she circulated around the room, she heard students articulating many well-rehearsed rules and procedures.

"You have to do that to both sides. . . ."

"You forgot the negative sign. . . ."

"You need to make improper fractions. . . ."

However, they weren't executing those rules and procedures accurately, and it was even more startling to Ms. Swanda that none of her students were considering the equation before beginning to solve it.

She called the class back together and asked the students to put their pencils down and revisit the equation. She asked her students if they thought it would be possible to solve this without pencil and paper. Gregory leaned back in his chair and raised his hand. He told the class that if you just looked at it first, it was easy to find x. He proceeded to describe how the stuff in the parentheses had to equal 4 because $-3 \cdot 4 = -12$. And if a number minus $\frac{1}{4}$ is 4, then x must be $4\frac{1}{4}$.

Ms. Swanda continued to facilitate a discussion to make sense of Gregory's strategy. And she quickly decided on one goal for her class this year—for them to break their compulsion to calculate.

Have you ever observed students like Ms. Swanda's, who dive into calculations and procedures without pausing to interpret the problem in front of them? And when a student does understand a problem and comes up with a strategy or shortcut for solving it (like Gregory), do other students listen in bewilderment, wondering how the classmate could even think of such a strategy? Although the student's thinking may be deeply rooted in mathematical structure, classmates often think the shortcut came out of left field or is some kind of mathematical magic.

The Contemplate Then Calculate reasoning routine both fights against students' rush to calculate and explicitly develops their capacity to notice and make use of mathematical structure (CCSS Standards for Mathematical Practice 7 [National Governors Association Center for Best Practices, Council of Chief State School Officers 2010]) to solve a problem. When students develop structural thinking, they are less likely to jump to rules and procedures and more likely to interpret structural features in a problem and use them to better understand it and develop a relevant and efficient solution strategy.

What Does It Mean to "Think Structurally"?

As with all mathematical thinking, we can identify structural thinking in what we attend to as we approach a mathematical problem situation, in what we ask ourselves, and in the resultant actions we take. We are thinking structurally when we pay attention to how number and space are organized and to the rules for operating within number and space. We ask ourselves questions that orient toward mathematical structure, like *What do I notice that might be mathematically important? How can I chunk this expression/representation to make sense of it? How can I change the form of this number/ expression/shape to surface the underlying structure?* And we think structurally when we chunk expressions, shapes, or other mathematical objects; when we change the form of a number, expression, or visual; and when we make connections between and among representations and mathematical ideas. Figure 4–1 summarizes what we attend to, key questions we can ask ourselves, and actions we can take when we approach mathematical problems with structural thinking.

Structural thinkers value the connections between and among mathematical ideas and look to apply the same structural thinking in a variety of mathematical contexts: analyzing visuals, interpreting graphs, solving equations, rewriting expressions, and so on.

Chunk

Finding the area of a composite figure is one situation where structural thinking applies. When structural thinkers find the area of a composite figure, they may look for chunks they know they can find the area of and chunks that are the same size so that they can easily add them together.

Let's explore an example of chunking by looking at the area of the irregular shape in Figure 4–2.

If you are thinking and reasoning structurally, then you . . .

ATTEND to

The Organization and Properties of Number and Space

ASK Yourself

- Is this behaving like something else I know?
- How can I use properties to uncover structure?
- How can I change the form to make it easier to work with?
- How can I "chunk" this to make sense of it?
- How can I connect this to math I know?

ACT

- Chunk complicated objects.
- Connect math ideas and representations.
- Change the form of objects.
- Recall and use properties, rules of operations, and geometric relationships.
- Shift perspective.

Figure 4–1

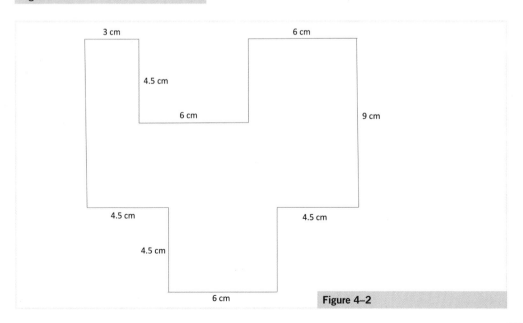

Figure 4–2

Structural thinkers might find the area by chunking the shape into four nonsquare rect-angles with known dimensions whose areas can be calculated and combined, as shown in Figure 4–3.

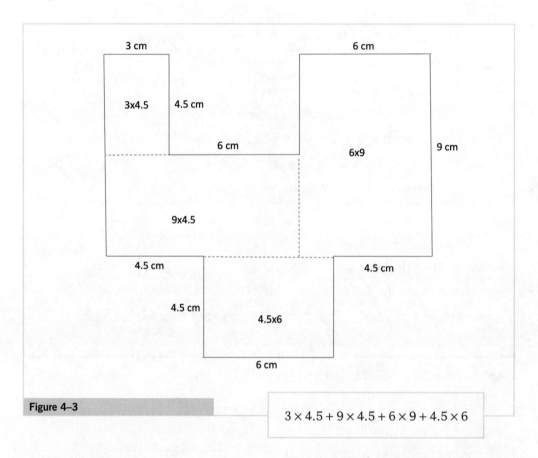

Figure 4–3

$$3 \times 4.5 + 9 \times 4.5 + 6 \times 9 + 4.5 \times 6$$

Or structural thinkers might look for same-size chunks by chunking the irregular shape into four nonsquare rectangles with the same dimensions (6 by 4.5) and a remaining nonsquare rectangle, as shown in Figure 4–4.

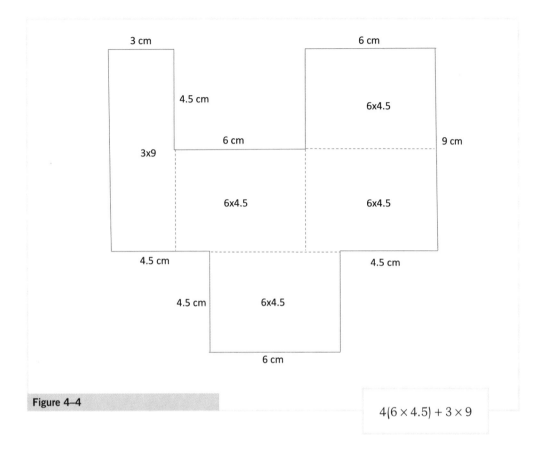

Figure 4–4

$$4(6 \times 4.5) + 3 \times 9$$

Similarly, when structural thinkers work with algebraic expressions, they look for chunks that are the same so that they can operate with them efficiently, avoiding detailed calculations and potential errors. When they see an expression like this:

$$4(12x + 1) - 2(12x + 1) + 5(12x + 1)$$

they notice the $(12x + 1)$ chunk rather than distributing the 4, the −2, and the 5 and collecting like terms, getting seven chunks of $(12x + 1)$ or $7(12x + 1)$.

Change

When structural thinkers look to change the form of a visual, expression, or other mathematical object, they often look for "friendly" numbers, shapes, or expressions that are *close* to the mathematical object, and then they change the form while attending to rules and properties.

For example, see Figure 4–5. Structural thinkers change the form by rearranging the parts of the figure, all the while maintaining total area. In this case, they see the "empty" 4.5-by-6 rectangle, and fill it with a rectangle with the same dimensions that extends outward. In doing so, they've changed the form to make a new rectangle that is 9 by 15 and are left to multiply 9×15.

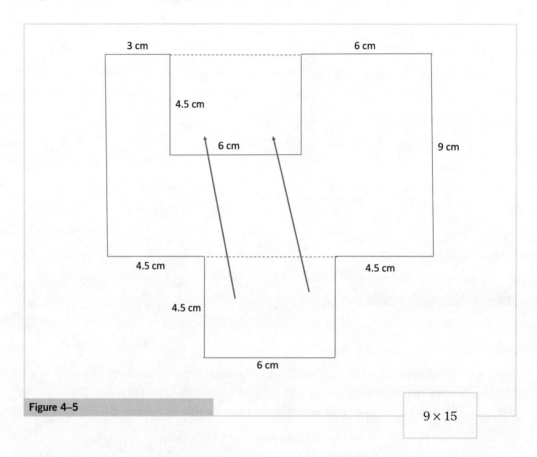

Figure 4–5

Similarly, structural thinkers would likely not use the standard algorithm to approach a multiplication task like 87×5. They might mentally calculate the product by applying properties (here, the commutative property of multiplication) to change the form of the expression to 5×87. They might then continue to change the form of one of the numbers to make it easier to work with. Perhaps they would change 87 to $80 + 7$, and then apply the distributive property by multiplying 5×80 and 5×7 and adding the resulting products.

Connect

Structural thinkers make connections between and among mathematical ideas and use those connections to deepen their understanding of the mathematics at hand. When structural thinkers are connecting to math they know, they might look at an expression like $3(x + 4)$ and interpret it by connecting it to what they know about multiplication. Perhaps the expression represents 3 groups of $(x + 4)$, connecting to multiplication as repeated addition. Perhaps the expression represents the dimensions of a rectangle that has dimensions of 3 and $(x + 4)$, connecting the expression to what they know about area and two-dimensional multiplication. In both cases, structural thinkers interpret $3(x + 4)$, rather than operating on it by distributing the 3. (Although learning the process of distributing is important, it is not the only way to make sense of the expression.) Or, when first presented with expressions involving x^2, they think about what they know about square numbers—that they are a number multiplied by itself, and that they form the shape of a square visually. In contrast, students who don't yet think structurally may only interpret x^2 as a variable with a little two to the upper right, or x to the second power.

Structural thinkers seek connections between and among operations as well. Rather than considering addition as a set of procedures to follow depending on the "type" of numbers you are adding, structural thinkers view addition as an operation that remains consistent regardless of the number set at hand. That is, structural thinkers add the same things to the same things whether they are adding ones to ones, hundredths to hundredths, x's to x's, $\frac{1}{4}$s to $\frac{1}{4}$s, $(x + 5)$s to $(x + 5)$s, or $\sin x$ to $\sin x$. And if the objects they'd like to add don't appear the same, they think about changing the form by asking themselves whether they can make the objects alike. When they look at $\frac{1}{3} + \frac{2}{9}$, they ask themselves, *Can I change the form of either $\frac{1}{3}$ or $\frac{2}{9}$ so that I can add them?* and it turns out they can. They ask themselves the same question when they look at $x^2 + 2x$, but they are unable to change the form to add x^2 and $2x$.

Similarly, students may connect the idea of changing the form to fill in negative space (as shown in Figure 4–5) to addition/subtraction strategies (e.g., $97 + 103$ can be calculated by "filling" the 97 to 100, and adding $100 + 100$) or to the process of completing the square, when an expression is adjusted to make it a perfect square.

Positioning Students to Think Structurally

Two ways to prompt structural thinking are to stop and notice mathematically important features and to develop shortcuts based in mathematical structure. For example, if students stop to notice something about the problem $1,001 - 999$, it is highly unlikely that they would start applying the standard algorithm. They would be much more inclined to consider the distance between these numbers, how they connect to friendly numbers, or that we could express each of them as one away from 1,000. For students to apply structural thinking to a variety of mathematical situations, we need to develop students' capacity to attend to and articulate their noticings.

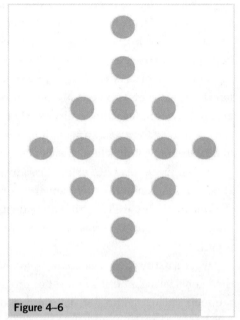

Before reading further, take a few moments to think structurally about the following tasks. Pause to notice structural features that will help you find elegant solution strategies based in mathematical structure. Try to chunk, change the form, and connect to math you know to solve them. We'll dig deeper into some of these tasks throughout this chapter.

1. What do you notice that might be mathematically important about Figure 4–6? Once you have a few noticings, use one or more of them to develop a shortcut to find the total number of dots without counting each one individually.

Figure 4–6

2. What do you notice about the expression in Figure 4–7? Once you have a few noticings, use one or more of them to develop a shortcut to find the value of the expression.

$$5 - 1 + 5 - 2 + 5 - 3 + 5 - 4$$

Figure 4–7

3. What do you notice about the equation in Figure 4–8? Once you have a few noticings, use one or more of them to develop a shortcut to find the value of x.

$$5(x + 3.5) - 3(\tfrac{7}{2} + x) + 1 = 17$$

Figure 4–8

After repeated experiences that emphasize noticings and shortcuts based in mathematical structure, students will begin to view mathematics as interconnected and as a discipline that makes sense. They'll realize they are applying the same kinds of thinking—chunking, changing the form, and connecting mathematical ideas and representations—regardless of the topic or unit of study.

An Overview of the Contemplate Then Calculate Reasoning Routine

In the Contemplate Then Calculate reasoning routine, students work together to develop shortcuts based in mathematical structure. This routine develops students' capacity to chunk and change complicated objects to make them easier to work with and leverage the connections between different math concepts and representations. In addition, it interrupts students' impulse to calculate and helps them develop the productive habit of pausing and noticing important mathematical features. After repeatedly engaging in the routine, students develop a robust understanding of mathematical structure and are able to apply their structural thinking outside of the routine.

The Steps of the Routine

Part 1: The Contemplate Then Calculate routine begins with an introduction to the routine, including a structural thinking goal.

Part 2: Students then put their pencils down and notice structural elements of a mathematical object—a visual, an arithmetic operation, an equation, or a graph—and share their noticings.

Part 3: Students then work with a partner and use their noticings to find a counting/calculating/solving shortcut by chunking the object, changing the form of it to make it easier to operate or calculate with, and/or connecting to mathematics they know that they can leverage in a shortcut.

Part 4: Then, in the full group, the teacher facilitates a discussion based on students' strategies, and students dig into the shortcuts and the structural thinking that underlies them.

Part 5: Finally, all the structural thinking that has been developed is solidified during the meta-reflection process as students reflect on how they developed their structural thinking and how they might use it in future problems.

Part 1: Launch the Routine

When launching the routine, the teacher identifies the thinking goal for the routine and reviews the steps. It is critical that students understand that the goal is to notice mathematical features that highlight structure and lead to structural thinking and that it extends beyond the content standard of the math task at hand; the broader goal is to develop mathematical thinking that is applicable to a wide variety of problems and contexts.

Steps for Part 1

1. Display and explain the thinking goal that outlines what students will learn and why they are learning it. For example, you might say, "Today we are going to develop our inner mathematicians. As mathematicians, we think structurally by chunking, changing the form, and/or connecting to math we know. Then, we are going to use our structural thinking to find a calculation shortcut."

2. Display and share the flow and format of the routine. You might say something like, "We will start by contemplating—noticing what might be mathematically important about today's task. Then you'll work with a partner to develop a shortcut, we'll share and discuss shortcuts in the full group, and finally, we'll reflect on structural thinking so that we can use it again in a different problem situation." There will be time in the parts that follow for more specific instructions and details.

Part 2: Notice

In the second part of the routine, the focus is on interpreting a mathematical object. The teacher poses an AYQ to support students' sense making ("What do I notice that might be mathematically important?") and then flashes a task similar to the ones on page 78 for two to three seconds, enough time to notice some features but not enough time to begin acting upon the task. Students work to notice what might be mathematically important and share their noticings with a partner and in the full group. The teacher records the noticings publicly so that all students have access to them throughout their work in the routine.

"Flashing" the task is very intentional. Doing so pauses student thinking and forces students to stay in the noticings, rather than to proceed immediately with a solution strategy. Students aren't given enough time to solve, calculate, or otherwise act on the task; they are only given enough time to see what they notice. The task then disappears so that the class can generate a list of noticings. Doing so develops a habit of mind of contemplating before calculating—slowing down to make sense of the task rather than diving into calculations and procedures. Structural thinkers often pause before putting pencil to paper, and this routine develops that habit in students.

Steps for Part 2

1. Frame the noticing process for students, particularly if the routine is new for them. You might say, "You'll see a task for only a couple of seconds. Your job is just to notice what might be mathematically important, and the task will return later. So, make sure your pencils are down and you can see the board." Ensure that all students can see the board before flashing the task. This framing becomes less and less necessary after multiple engagements in the routine.

2. Allow individual think time. Pose the AYQ to orient and support student thinking ("What do I notice that might be mathematically important?") and flash the task for 1–3 seconds. It's always better to provide less time than more time. Students can generate additional noticings throughout the routine, but if they see the task for too long, their compulsion to calculate may kick in and it will be difficult to elicit structural thinking.

3. Have the students work in pairs. Immediately, prompt students to turn to their partner and share their noticing, using the sentence starter and question "I noticed _____" and "What did you notice?" If the teacher takes too much time transitioning to pairs, students may lose the noticing they are holding in their short-term memory.

4. As students turn and talk, circulate to listen and select a few noticings you'd like students to share in the full group.

5. Share out. Have specific students share noticings and record them for all students to see and potentially use as they develop shortcuts. Ideally, you've noted which students are sharing noticings and the order in which you'd like the noticings shared.

Part 3: Develop Shortcuts

In this part of the routine, students work together to use one or more of the noticings that the teacher elicited and recorded (or even a noticing that has not yet been shared) and develop a shortcut together.

Steps for Part 3

1. Explain to students that they will work *together* to find a shortcut. It might help to contrast collaborative sense making through partner work with sharing answers. As you give instructions, ensure the task is not visible to students or they will not be listening to you.

2. When you've finished giving the directions for partner work, reproject or post the task for students to see and point to as they work together to find a shortcut.

3. Have students work in pairs. As students develop and discuss their shortcut strategies with their partners, circulate and listen to identify two or three lines of reasoning to discuss in the full group. Select a variety of shortcuts so students can consider the strategies used and then surface and leverage the underlying structure of each one. Decide the sequence of strategies based on the student thinking in the room and the mathematical goal. We will discuss this decision-making process later in the chapter.

Part 4: Discuss Shortcuts

The full-group discussion serves to make the thinking in the room public so that every student's structural thinking develops. The full-group discussion involves the Four Rs (repeat, rephrase, reword, and record) so that ideas are heard, developed, and refined. Students share and rephrase using specific sentence frames to support language production and also to focus on the structural thinking. As students share and rephrase strategies, the teacher annotates the original task to support student sense making and provide visual residue of the thinking. Students dive deeper into the thinking when the teacher poses turn-and-talks.

Steps for Part 4

1. Prompt the first partnership you've selected to share their thinking, starting with "We noticed _____ so we _____" or "We knew _____ so we _____." Prompt the other students to listen carefully to the strategy and be prepared to rephrase it using the sentence frames "They noticed _____ so they _____" or "They knew _____ so they _____."

2. As students begin to share, the teacher points and gestures to the math task as a multimodal support for students as they listen. Gesturing also helps ensure that you are hearing the idea in the way that students intended and prepares you to annotate in a way that highlights the structural thinking that drives the strategy. (Read more about why the teacher does the pointing and gesturing in the FAQ section on page 98.)

3. Ask students to rephrase the thinking, using the sentence frames "They noticed _____ so they _____" or "They knew _____ so they _____."

4. As classmates rephrase the shortcut, annotate the task with color, symbols, and language to highlight structural thinking—chunking, changing the form, and/or connecting mathematical ideas.

5. Decide whether students would benefit from delving further into the approach, and if so, pose a question about the mathematical structure of the shortcut strategy—the validity of the approach or the underlying properties, rules of operations, and/or relationships that students used. Provide a few seconds of private think time and then prompt students to turn and talk as appropriate to process and make sense of the ideas and questions you raise. Listen in to partner conversations to help inform how you will facilitate the sharing of responses, and then select student pairs to share in the full group.

6. Repeat this sensemaking process with additional shortcut strategies (annotating on a clean copy of the image) that provide or extend new structural insights as time permits.

Part 5: Reflect on Structural Thinking

Last, and definitely not least, the routine ends with a reflection that will help students approach future problems. If time is running short, it is better to discuss fewer shortcuts and save time for the reflection than to shortchange the reflection process.

Steps for Part 5

1. Allow individual write time. Remind students why they engaged in the routine (e.g., "to learn to think structurally," "to use what you know about the way numbers and operations work to find calculation shortcuts") and emphasize the importance of reflecting on their thinking. Explain that they will reflect by writing individually, sharing with a partner, and then sharing in the full group. Provide students with sentence starters and frames to focus their reflection (e.g., "To find a shortcut look for _____," "Noticing _____ helped me calculate quickly because _____," or "Knowing _____ comes in handy when calculating quickly because _____"). Ask students to select one of the sentence starters/frames, and then write individually. As they write, circulate, but confer minimally; prompt a student to elaborate with details or examples, but do not engage in discussion about their meta-reflections. Begin to select reflections that highlight important elements of structural thinking and that might be valuable for peers to hear.

2. Have students share their written reflections with their partners. Listen in as you continue to identify reflections that will be important to share in the full group.

3. Share and record. Prompt preselected students to share their reflection(s) with the whole class and record the reflections. This public record serves as residue in the classroom so that students may refer to it later and use it as an anchor chart for structural thinking.

Essential Strategies in the Routine

As in our other routines, all five essential strategies (annotation, AYQs, sentence frames and starters, the Four Rs, and turn-and-talk) are integrated in Contemplate Then Calculate (see Figure 4–9). They all focus students' attention on structural thinking and support them in developing it, but annotation and sentence frames and starters play a central role in capturing and communicating structural thinking.

Contemplate Then Calculate

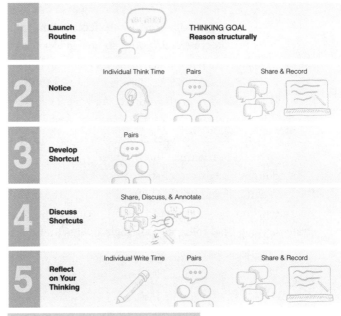

1 Launch Routine — (VOTE OUTRANK) — THINKING GOAL / Reason structurally

2 Notice — Individual Think Time / Pairs / Share & Record

3 Develop Shortcut — Pairs

4 Discuss Shortcuts — Share, Discuss, & Annotate

5 Reflect on Your Thinking — Individual Write Time / Pairs / Share & Record

Figure 4–9

Annotation

Contemplate Then Calculate uses annotation during the full-class discussion (Part 4) to connect what students are saying to what they are seeing, to highlight students' structural thinking, and ultimately to develop and solidify structural thinking—how students chunk, change the form, and/or make connections between and among mathematical representations and concepts. In addition, annotation provides residue of the structural thinking so that students may refer to it later in the discussion or even another day. Although the purpose of annotation within Contemplate Then Calculate is to highlight structural thinking, recall the benefits we discussed in Chapter 2.

Consider the annotation in Figure 4–10 of the task $5 - 1 + 5 - 2 + 5 - 3 + 5 - 4$. You can imagine all that students may continue to glean from it both during the discussion and even after it has finished. What noticings and structural features can you infer from the annotation in Figure 4–10?

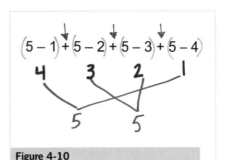

Figure 4-10

The annotation reveals attention to operations, with the purple arrows pointing to the addition signs, chunking the subtraction pieces by adding parentheses, and then changing the form by applying properties of addition to add 4 and 1, then 3 and 2, indicated by the red line segments.

I noticed...
so I knew...
so I looked for..
...connects to...
because...

Sentence Frames and Starters

Although we know that sentence frames and starters support students in general—to provide organization for thoughts, to provide language to get started, to give students a running start when they are hesitant to begin sharing, and so on—in Contemplate Then Calculate, the sentence frames and starters place a laser-like focus on structural thinking. The sentence frame "We noticed _____ so we _____" steers students to their initial noticings rather than what they did or what answer they found. As we previously discussed, these initial noticings are the foundations for structural thinking. A similar sentence frame, "They noticed _____ so they _____," focuses classmates' attention on the structural thinking because they will use it to rephrase the shortcut.

In addition, the essential strategies provide teachers opportunities to put the three teaching shifts (focus on thinking, step out of the middle, and support productive struggle) into action. So, as you read the following vignette, pay attention to how the essential strategies play dual roles, supporting students and teachers.

Contemplate Then Calculate in Action

In this vignette, we visit Ms. Clark's sixth-grade class, focusing on the task in Figure 4–11. Before reading further, take a moment to interpret the visual. Ask yourself, *What do I notice that might be mathematically important?* Then, use one of your noticings to count all the dots without counting each one individually.

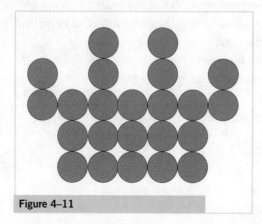

Figure 4–11

[CLASSROOM SNAPSHOT]

Ms. Clark's Sixth-Grade Math Class

Ms. Clark launches Contemplate Then Calculate by framing the thinking goal (to use the structure of a visual to find a counting shortcut) and reviewing the agenda. She flashes the task, prompts students to share their noticings with a partner, and shares a few in the full group.

Let's jump in at the beginning of Part 3. Ms. Clark has recorded the following list of noticings. We've included the names of the students in each partnership so you can refer to them later.

We Noticed . . .

Purple circles (Giuliana & Harris)

A spaceship (Katya & Conor)

A rectangular chunk (Dwaina & Liz)

Some columns were longer than the others (Maria & Eric)

? Symmetry ? (Kit & Chelsey)

▶ *Notice that Ms. Clark elicited and recorded two noticings that may not at first glance seem mathematically important—"purple circles" and "a spaceship." However, it is very important that the unit students are counting (i.e., purple circles) is the same size and shape, which might emerge during students' discussion and provide fodder to articulate the importance of "same-size chunks." Students may use the spaceship noticing as a means to support their communication and later develop precision in their mathematical language. Ms. Clark is starting with the student thinking in the room, all the while keeping her structural thinking goal in mind.*

PART 3: DEVELOP SHORTCUTS

Ms. Clark gives students instructions for the next stage.

Ms. Clark: When I reproject the task, you and your partner should use one of the noticings we shared, or maybe one that hasn't yet been shared, to find a counting shortcut. It might be helpful if you select a noticing together so that you can work together as you develop your strategy. (*Reprojects task*)

▶ *Ms. Clark sets the stage for students to be working together, a precursor to stepping out of the middle.*

Conor: I thought it looked like a spaceship, so maybe we can use the body of the spaceship.

Katya: OK, so that (*pointing to outline a rectangle*) looks like a rectangle like Dwaina and Liz said. It's a 3-by-5 rectangle.

Conor: I see that, too. So that's 3×5 or 15.

Katya: And, if you add in the arms of the spaceship, there are 2 dots on each of the 4 arms. One arm of 2 on each side and 2 arms of 2 on the top.

Conor: OK, so that's 4 groups of 2, or 8.

Katya: And 15 + 8 is 23.

> ▶ *Sharing noticings publicly supports productive struggle. Notice that Katya and Conor leveraged and built onto Liz and Dwaina's noticing to find their own counting shortcut. Their classmates' noticing provided them an entry into the problem that they otherwise wouldn't have had.*

Kit: OK, so I think it *is* symmetrical. The line of symmetry is actually those 3 dots in the middle. (*Gesturing to the center column*)

Chelsey: Me too. So if we find the total on the left, we can double it because of the symmetry and then add the 3 in the middle.

Kit: Well, one side is 10, so the other side is 10, plus that 3. So 23.

Chelsey: Wait, how do you know one side is 10?

Kit: I moved the 2 dots onto the 3 dots to make 5, and the next column already had 5. And, 5 + 5 is 10.

Chelsey: Oh, I see. That's cool.

> ▶ *Notice that Kit and Chelsey confirmed their initial noticing by finding evidence within the visual. They continued to co-construct a shortcut and held each other accountable throughout the process; Chelsey pressed for evidence when Kit claimed each side had 10 dots. Both students are engaged in mathematical thinking and justification, the impact of Ms. Clark stepping out of the middle.*

Dwaina: Now we can find the dimensions of the rectangular chunk we saw.

Liz: Yes, it's 3 by 5, so that's 15.

Dwaina: And if we look at the extras, there are 4 groups of 2. But now I see a larger rectangle we could make. If we slide the left group of 2 up and over and the right group of 2 up and over, we almost have a new rectangle. We'd be missing 2.

Liz: Oh, so we could find the total by doing $5 \times 5 - 2$.

....

Maria: What if we try to make the columns the same length?

Eric: What do you mean? Like make them all 5s?

Maria: I think that would work for the 2 columns on the left and the 2 columns on the right.

Eric: OK, so we'd have two 5s, a 3, and two more 5s.

> ▶ *These two partnerships continue to build on their own noticings, ensuring they understand each other's thinking. Notice how each partner contributes to the strategy and Ms. Clark is not interrupting or adding on.*

As she listens in, Ms. Clark chooses strategies to share in the full group. She wants to focus student attention on the strategies that involve changing the form of the object because changing the form is the least developed aspect of structural thinking for her students.

PART 4: DISCUSS SHORTCUTS

Ms. Clark brings the class back together and prompts three partnerships to share their counting shortcuts. After sharing two others, she invites Dwaina and Liz to share.

Ms. Clark: So, let's take a look at one more counting shortcut. Dwaina and Liz, could you share your strategy, starting with what you noticed? And, remember, if you are in the audience, you should be listening to what they noticed and be prepared to rephrase their strategy using the sentence frame "They noticed _____ so they _____."

I noticed...
so I knew...
so I looked for...
...connects to...
because...

Dwaina: We noticed the rectangular shape, so we tried to make the largest rectangle we could. Just like Kit and Chelsey's strategy, we slid the 2 dots on the left up and to the right, and the 2 dots on the right up and to the left.

Ms. Clark: Like this? (*Points and gestures*)

Dwaina: Yeah, and then we almost had a complete 5-by-5 rectangle, or actually it would be a square I guess. So, we did $5 \times 5 - 2$.

Ms. Clark: Who can rephrase Dwaina and Liz's strategy starting with what they noticed? Conor?

Conor: They noticed the rectangle and the 2s just like we did, but they changed it into a larger rectangle, or 5-by-5 square, but it wasn't complete, so they had to take 2 away. It's like they fenced it in.

▶ *Notice how Conor uses the sentence frame to rephrase Dwaina and Liz's thinking, starting with their noticing, which he and his partner also used. However, he was able to rephrase their strategy (and further his own structural thinking) after listening and watching Ms. Clark point and gesture.*

Ms. Clark annotates as Conor rephrases, and the image looks like Figure 4–12.

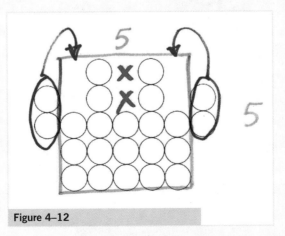

Figure 4–12

Ms. Clark: I have a question for y'all. If you wanted to use this strategy again, what is it that you'd look for to make sure it would work? (*She pauses, providing some private think time.*) Turn and talk to your partners. (*She circulates to listen to student thinking and make decisions about what she'd like shared in the full group.*)

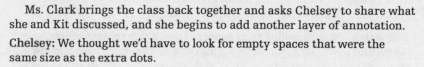

▶ *Ms. Clark chose to dig into this strategy a bit more through a turn-and-talk to make the thinking explicit for all to understand and use again. Students are supported as they make sense of and extrapolate from their classmate's short-cut—they have private think time, an opportunity to talk with a partner, and can reference the visual residue left from the annotation.*

Ms. Clark brings the class back together and asks Chelsey to share what she and Kit discussed, and she begins to add another layer of annotation.

Chelsey: We thought we'd have to look for empty spaces that were the same size as the extra dots.

Ms. Clark: Katya, can you rephrase what Chelsey said in your own words?

Katya: Yeah, she would see how many extra dots there were and then look to see if there were that many extra spaces. She could only add extras in if she could take them away from somewhere else.

Dante: I'd like to add on to what Chelsey and Katya said because they could also look for empty spaces to fill in and subtract if they couldn't really fill them in with the dots. That's why you have to subtract the 2 from 5×5.

The final annotation looks like Figure 4–13.

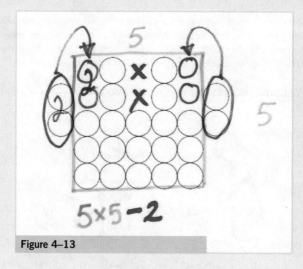

Figure 4–13

▶ *When Katya rephrases Chelsey's thought, she is beginning to own it for herself. Verbalizing the idea helps her to understand it, allows others to hear it again, and positions all students to apply that line of thinking in another context, as evidenced by Dante's capacity to add on to Katya and Chelsey's thinking.*

I noticed...
so I knew...
so I looked for...
...connects to...
because...

PART 5: META-REFLECTION

The final step in the routine is for students to reflect on the thinking they've developed in a write-pair-share.

Ms. Clark frames the meta-reflection, connecting it to the goal of the lesson, and tells students to select one of the prompts provided.

- To find a shortcut, look for _____.
- Noticing _____ helped me count quickly because _____.
- Knowing _____ comes in handy when counting quickly because _____.

She then sends students off to write individually, and begins observing student responses. Once she sees most students have completed their reflection, she asks them to share them with their partners. As students do so, Ms. Clark listens in. She pulls the class back together and prompts four or five students to share their meta-reflections while she records them in a public and permanent way.

Ms. Clark: Liz, could you share your reflection?

Liz: Sure. To find a shortcut look for friendly shapes like we did, but also symmetry because then you can just find $\frac{1}{2}$ of the total and double it.

▶ *Ms. Clark purposely selected Liz's meta-reflection because Liz referred to other partnerships' noticing and strategy. Ms. Clark implicitly sends the message that learning from classmates is valuable and sets herself up to continue stepping out of the middle.*

The Teacher's Role

Throughout Contemplate Then Calculate, teachers have the opportunity to enact the three shifts: focus on thinking, step out of the middle, and support productive struggle. In this example, Ms. Clark's shifts were not always obvious, but they were critical.

Focus on Thinking

From articulating a thinking goal to sharing meta-reflections, Ms. Clark made decisions throughout to focus on thinking. Ms. Clark anticipated (and really hoped!) that students would notice empty spaces so that they'd be inclined to change the form to count efficiently. Students did notice empty spaces, but in a different way than Ms. Clark anticipated. So, she authentically listened to students' noticings and worked from what she heard to highlight multiple ways to chunk, change the form, and connect mathematical ideas. She did not infuse her own strategy, which would undermine the valuable student strategies. She started with the thinking in the room and worked from there to develop structural thinking in all students.

Step Out of the Middle

Ms. Clark took herself out of the middle. She did not engage in conversations with partnerships as she listened to noticings, shortcut strategies, or meta-reflections. She took in ideas and made decisions. She repeatedly prompted students to rephrase each other's thinking, facilitated student-to-student discourse, and resisted the temptation to repeat students' ideas herself and/or to jump into the conversation. As a result, students listened authentically to each other in partnerships and in the full group.

Support Productive Struggle

Contemplate Then Calculate structures productive struggle into its design: pausing to notice, sharing noticings publicly, providing processing time with partners to develop shortcuts. In addition, Ms. Clark posed a purposeful turn-and-talk to dig more deeply into a particular strategy. At that point, students had made sense of the task, had heard the strategy and a rephrase of the strategy, and were poised to delve further into the underlying structural thinking of the strategy.

Planning and Implementing Contemplate Then Calculate

Contemplate Then Calculate is most effective when teachers focus on structural thinking throughout the planning and implementation process. When teachers carefully anticipate student thinking and how to highlight it throughout the routine, they position themselves to make in-the-moment decisions that maintain a laserlike focus on students' structural thinking.

Getting Started

Choosing Tasks

We recommend beginning with familiar content around which to think structurally. Doing so will shift the cognitive load from the content to the structural thinking and the predictable design of the routine, so students can focus on learning the routine and on structural thinking. Try starting with three visual pattern tasks followed by two number tasks, and then moving on to current content in your curriculum. Quickly counting the number of items in a visual pattern is not only something that all students can do, it naturally encourages them to chunk the visual, change its form, and connect to math they know to find a shortcut. When the tasks shift to number calculations, students will see how these very same actions happen with numbers and operations as well.

The tasks on page 78 all work well in Contemplate Then Calculate—visual patterns, complicated number tasks, and/or algebraic equations. You can explore more of them at fosteringmathpractices.com. We've vetted these tasks, so you can be confident they will prompt structural thinking. Twitter is also a great place to find tasks as many teachers around the country are developing their own—look for the hashtag #CthenC.

To find or create your own, look through your own textbook and teaching materials. When considering a task for Contemplate Then Calculate, ask yourself the following three questions:

- Are there multiple mathematical features to notice (in a short time) about the task?
- Does the task invite structural thinking (i.e., chunking, changing, and connecting)?
- Is there more than one shortcut strategy?

If the answer to these three questions is yes, then the task is a good one.

Introducing the Routine

When first using Contemplate Then Calculate, focus on establishing the predictable nature of the routine. We suggest having the same group of students experience the routine five times over the course of 1–2 weeks. Make sure you get through all parts of the routine each time. Doing so will ensure that your students and you internalize the routine's flow and purpose. Once the routine is established, use it whenever it makes sense. It will feel like returning to an old friend.

We think starting the year with a series of Contemplate Then Calculate lessons is a great way to establish a classroom culture of collaborative sense making that engages every student. Doing so sends the message that every student is a math thinker and has mathematical ideas worth considering. In addition to establishing a focus on mathematical thinking, starting the year with Contemplate Then Calculate will help your students build habits of mathematical discourse. Finally, starting the year with a sequence of visual and number tasks provides students a bit of review and you a formative assessment opportunity.

Preparing for the Routine

Since the designs for learning in Contemplate Then Calculate stay the same each time, preparing to facilitate the routine means being clear about the learning goal, familiarizing yourself with the particular task you have chosen, anticipating students' thinking, and considering how you will annotate the task to capture student thinking and support student discourse.

1. Articulate the math thinking goal. To start, the math thinking goal will be a general structural thinking goal like "Find a calculation shortcut by chunking, changing the form, or connecting to math you know." As students begin to develop language for chunking, changing the form, and connecting to math they know, you can provide more specific thinking goals (e.g., "Chunk algebraic equations to solve efficiently" or "Change the form of geometric representations to calculate measurements").

2. Do the math. Notice what is mathematically important about the task you've chosen. Then use those noticings to develop as many shortcut strategies as you can.

3. Anticipate student thinking. Think about what students will notice about the task and how they might describe their noticings. Think about what shortcuts students might develop, and the structural underpinnings of the shortcuts. How do the shortcuts provide evidence of chunking, changing the form, and connecting mathematical ideas? Think about what student meta-reflections might be—anticipating exemplary student reflections will help you make decisions when facilitating the discussion. You can choose to highlight or dig into specific strategies that will plant seeds for the ideas captured in the meta-reflections you've anticipated.

4. Annotate shortcut strategies. Practice annotating the task to highlight student thinking and underscore the lesson goal while students share and discuss their shortcuts.

5. Walk through the presentation slides (available on fosteringmathpractices.com) and insert the goal you've crafted and the task you've selected. Projecting a similar slide deck each time supports the routineness and provides a visual representation of the cues and prompts throughout the routine.

6. Tweak the language of the directions, sentence frames and starters, and the meta-reflections based on your task (count the number of squares/circles, determine the value of this expression, find a calculation shortcut, and so on) and your goal (chunking, changing the form, and connecting to math you know).

   Note: The AYQ "What do I notice that might be mathematically important?" doesn't change. The sentence frames "I noticed _____," "What did you notice?," "We noticed _____ so we _____," and "They noticed _____ so they _____" also remain the same regardless of the task and goal.

Resources including tasks, presentation slides, and a planning document can be found on fosteringmathpractices.com.

Decisions in the Moment

Throughout Contemplate Then Calculate, teachers serve as facilitators of student thinking. They step out of the middle and keep a laser-like focus on structural thinking. To do so, they make key decisions as they surface student thinking and process it in relation to the goal of the lesson. They need to listen carefully to as many student-developed strategies as possible and decide which ones they will share and in which order. In Contemplate Then Calculate, teachers don't have a lot of time to make these decisions. Here are a few tips and questions to guide the decision-making processes.

Taking in Student Ideas

To listen to as many student pairs as possible, position yourself in the room so that you can monitor multiple partnerships at once. Often, you can hear snippets of a strategy and connect it to one you anticipated during the planning process. That allows you to swiftly move to another area of the room.

Because students are engaged in a task that is projected or on the board, they are looking up, together, in a common direction. When they point or gesture to support their conversations, their hands are often in the air in front of them, and their movements indicate the essence of their strategy. So, watch student gestures as a means to take in students' thinking.

Selecting and Sequencing Student Ideas

As you take in student thinking, think about which strategies you will select to be shared in the full group and in what order. This decision-making depends on your goals as well as the thinking you hear in the room. Here are a few tips to support your decision-making process:

- If your goal is to share one illustration of each pillar of structural thinking—chunking, changing the form, and connecting to math you know—then it doesn't matter which specific strategy you hear, just that you've heard a strategy that provides a clear example of each. Oftentimes, the chunking strategy is most accessible to students, so we start with that so that all students have access to the discussion as it builds. Changing the form is less concrete than chunking, as students envision moving numbers or mathematical objects to develop their shortcut, so we build up to that.

- Sometimes, there is a fairly common strategy in the room. It often makes sense to start with that strategy to establish a common understanding and provide access to all students. Then, students are positioned to move on to a strategy that requires more sense making and/or deeper analysis of the structural underpinnings of the strategy.

- Your goal may be to articulate the benefits of different ways to chunk a visual (same-size chunks, friendly shapes, largest chunk with the fewest leftovers, and so on). In that case, the order of the strategies is less important, but selecting varied chunking strategies is critical.

Analyzing Student Strategies

- While facilitating the full-group discussion, teachers mine one or more strategies for deeper analysis through a turn-and-talk. Developing that turn-and-talk in the moment can be challenging, but Contemplate Then Calculate includes a highly productive and transferable prompt: "What do you think they had to notice to use/develop this strategy?" Orienting to noticings is always a good reason to turn and talk!

Common Pitfalls

There are four pitfalls teachers often encounter when they first start using Contemplate Then Calculate. We have too! Common pitfalls include the following:

- cold calling
- focusing on answers
- trolling for a predetermined strategy
- serial conferring.

Cold Calling

One challenge when starting out with Contemplate Then Calculate is listening to a high volume of student thinking in a short period of time and making decisions in the moment about which student ideas to share and in what order. It's tempting to short-circuit the process and cold call students to share. However, doing so runs the risk of derailing the routine. For instance, depending on the task, there are sometimes key noticings that lead students to a specific shortcut. If that is the case, take care to save those noticings for last, or not at all. In the task in this chapter, one such noticing would be "two empty spaces." Similarly, the careful sequencing of shortcut strategies in the full-group discussion allows the teacher to strategically build understanding through the discussion. If a teacher randomly calls on a student who shares an abstract or unique strategy first, students will not have had the benefit of building understanding through strategies that are more commonly understood.

Focusing on the Answer

It is easy to fall into the trap of focusing on the answer rather than the thinking behind the answer. A shortcut often connotes getting a quick answer. However, in this routine the focus is not on the answer or even the steps of the shortcut strategy, but rather the structural thinking underlying the strategy. To avoid this pitfall, leverage the AYQ "What might be mathematically important?" and the sentence frames and starters designed to shift attention toward structural thinking. When in doubt, connect back to the noticings and identify the one that started the math thinking ball rolling.

Trolling for a Predetermined Strategy

We wrote earlier that an essential part of planning is to find as many shortcut strategies as possible for the task you chose. Revel in the range of strategies you find, but keep yourself from becoming wedded to a particularly interesting or elegant shortcut. You want to be open to the student thinking in the room, not impose one particular way to think about the problem on students. Resist the temptation to pursue a particular strategy, as doing so will prevent you from authentically listening to student thinking. Also resist the temptation to step in and share that super cool strategy you discovered. If you share a shortcut that was not in the room—even if it came from another class—it will diminish the student thinking and student-generated strategies in the room.

Serial Conferring

The routine moves quickly, and you will need to as well. Rather than touring the room pair by pair asking questions, position yourself centrally so that you can quickly eavesdrop on multiple partner conversations and then reposition yourself to listen in on another group. Keep in mind the following two goals:

- Know the range of student thinking in the room so that you can select and sequence student ideas for the full-group share.
- Provide space for students to co-construct math ideas.

Stepping to the side and providing students the time and space to work together will not only give you time to take in the student ideas in the room, but also sends the message to your students that they are capable, creative math thinkers.

Remember that because the routine is repeatable, it is forgiving. If you fall into one of these traps, don't worry. You will soon have another opportunity to lead Contemplate Then Calculate, and the next time you will be that much more mindful of avoiding the pitfall.

Frequently Asked Questions

How much time does Contemplate Then Calculate take?

The first few times, the routine can take upward of thirty minutes. Once you and your students become familiar with the flow, the directions tighten up, and the transitions become more succinct, you can complete the routine in fifteen minutes. Having said that, once the routine is familiar and your students have built some mathematical discourse stamina, you may choose to sit in the full-group discussion longer to drill deeper into a particular line of structural thinking or mathematical idea.

Where does Contemplate Then Calculate fit into my curriculum?

The short answer is anywhere you see an opportunity for students to make sense of mathematical structure or pause and notice before jumping into calculating. Content standards that have to do with mathematical structure often include the phrase "apply and extend." This phrase is a cue that you will be using the same math property or operation with a new mathematical object (e.g., "Apply and extend previous understandings of operations with fractions to add, subtract, multiply, and divide rational numbers"). Look for content standards that speak directly to structural thinking, such as expressions and equations standards like "View one or more parts of an expression as a single entity" (a chunk!) or "Apply the properties of operations to generate equivalent expressions" (changing the form!). Many teachers use Contemplate Then Calculate as a warm-up to develop structural thinking, and then encourage students to use that thinking throughout the ensuing lesson.

What do I do if I flash the task and students don't have any mathematical noticings?

They will. Often students do notice something mathematical but describe it at first in nonmathematical terms. Consider the task from Ms. Clark's class that we saw earlier. Throughout the routine, students rephrase and reword classmates' thinking, and their descriptive language will gain mathematical precision. You can highlight the mathematical language by adding these more precise descriptors (*array, rectangle, equal groups, symmetry,* and so on) to the list of noticings and/or the annotation. The next time students notice, they will look for these mathematical features and use more precise language in describing them. Students have mathematical ideas. It is our job to recognize them and provide students the opportunity to grow them.

What do I do if a student shares an incorrect shortcut strategy?

It happens, although much less frequently than you'd expect. The mistake is often a calculation mistake (e.g., adding 8 and 15 and getting 22 in the previous task) or a miscount (e.g., skip counting an extra set of 2 circles), not a structural thinking error. Typically, other students catch the mistake and tweak the shortcut. When this happens, highlight the important structural thinking and casually correct the calculation. The goal of Contemplate Then Calculate is to develop structural thinking, not to know the exact number of circles. Keep the focus on the goal and students' mathematical thinking.

Can I use this routine with word problems?
Making sense of problem situations is critical, and pausing to interpret them plays an essential role in that process. Experienced teachers have adapted the routine to use word problems at the center of Contemplate Then Calculate. Teachers also share with students that they can (and should!) apply the same reasoning process when approaching word problems: stopping to contemplate and interpret before acting. We also highly recommend using the Three Reads routine (described in *Routines for Reasoning*) to interpret and make sense of problem situations and important information.

Can students do the pointing/gesturing and annotation?
In this routine, teachers point, gesture, and annotate during the discussion. This multimodal support serves to highlight structural thinking connected to the goal of the lesson. While the original partnership shares their shortcut strategy, the teacher listens carefully to student thinking and points and gestures to support students, while simultaneously making decisions about how to annotate the idea. Although an experienced annotator may make the process look easy, it is complex and critical to the structural thinking goal of Contemplate Then Calculate. In the final chapter, we will provide activities to develop your annotation practice.

Can I provide students with pencil and paper?
It's tempting to give students paper to work on to develop their shortcut. We test-drove this during the development of the routine and found out (the hard way!) that when students have paper in front of them, they talk less, limiting the teacher's ability to listen and make decisions, and, more importantly, removing both the support that discourse provides students as well as the opportunity to develop and articulate their thinking verbally. Also, when students are up close to a task with a writing utensil in hand, they are more likely to give in to their compulsion to calculate, and they lose the opportunity to step back, notice, and look for and make use of structure.

REFLECT ON YOUR READING

1. Why is structural thinking important to develop in all students?

2. What about Contemplate Then Calculate and its embedded designs for interaction supports students with learning disabilities? English learners?

3. What might be the impact on students' thinking if they engage in Contemplate Then Calculate over time?

4. In the vignette, what moment stood out to you as being critical to engaging all students in structural thinking? Why/how was it critical?

5. What critical instruction shift (focusing on thinking, stepping out of the middle, or supporting productive struggle) will you focus on when you start facilitating Contemplate Then Calculate?

6. Which essential strategy (annotation, AYQs, Four Rs, sentence frames and starters, or turn-and-talk) will you work to develop as you begin facilitating Contemplate Then Calculate?

Design Your Own Reasoning Routine

In this chapter we pull back the curtain on our process for designing a reasoning routine. In doing so we hope that you will both better understand the critical role the essential strategies play in prompting the three instructional shifts in practice and be able to develop your own reasoning routines to support your work in creating a thinking classroom.

We begin by exploring inspirations for developing a reasoning routine, then offer a step-by-step development process, illustrating each step with examples from our routines. Throughout, we will unpack how we developed our latest routine, Analyzing Contexts and Models, which fosters students' capacity to model with mathematics (CCSS Standards for Mathematical Practice (SMP) 4 [National Governors Association Center for Best Practices, Council of Chief State School Officers 2010]).

Finding Your Inspiration

When we first started creating our routines, we wanted to craft learning opportunities that prompted and developed mathematical practices. Later, we found inspiration in the structured lesson designs and types of tasks found in various math curricula and texts that invited mathematical thinking and reasoning. All of these have at their core regularity and repetition—the foundation of a reasoning routine. A mathematical practice—or a practice of any kind—is by definition a routine and can only be developed through repetition. A predictable lesson layout that is repeated page after page offers regularity to leverage, as does a common task type.

Promoting a Mathematical Practice

We view the eight mathematical practices championed in the CCSS Standards for Mathematics (National Governors Association Center for Best Practices, Council of Chief State School Officers 2010) as critical habits of thinking and working that successful math doers bring to their math learning and problem solving. They need to be named and mindfully developed through regular, repeated exposure. Reasoning routines are our way of explicitly teaching a math practice and not just assuming (or hoping!) that because students were solving problems or building conceptual understanding, the practices would naturally follow. Thus, our routines begin with explicitly naming for students what the mathematical thinking they are developing looks like, engage them in an activity that prompts them to think in that way, and end with students articulating what they learned about thinking mathematically that they can bring to their future math doing. What math practice would you like your students to develop? Is there an aspect of mathematical thinking and reasoning you would like to become second nature for your students?

Capitalizing on a Common Task Type

Tasks that prompt mathematical thinking are finding their way into mathematics classrooms. For example, teachers and curriculum developers alike are making liberal use of high-cognitive-demand activities like Christopher Danielson's Which One Doesn't Belong?, Dan Meyer's Three-Act Math tasks, Fawn Nguyen's Visual Patterns, NCTM's Notice and Wonder, as well as old favorites like sorting activities and worked examples. The predictable design of these activities is a great jumping-off point for creating a reasoning routine. In fact, we created the Decide and Defend reasoning routine to leverage the influx of worked examples in recent curricula. Creating a predictable flow and set of designs for interaction around a type of task you use regularly in your teaching is a great way to repurpose something you are already using. What tasks do you use around which you could design a reasoning routine?

Leveraging a Lesson Design

Curriculum developers work hard to build consistency and predictability into the design of their learning materials. Although the structured layout of the materials can make them more visually appealing and help students and teachers navigate the pages, some design decisions specifically speak to productive ways of engaging students in the mathematics. The regular features resulting from these latter design decisions can inspire a reasoning routine. For example, the problem-centered nature of the CMP (Connected Mathematics Program) led to its seminal launch-explore-summarize lesson design. A critical feature of the lesson summary is orchestrating a discussion around carefully selected and sequenced work from student groups to surface and connect important mathematical concepts. This kind of discussion of the structural connections between and among the representations in student work formed the genesis of our Connecting Representations reasoning routine. A second example of a regular lesson design feature in a mathematics program that spawned an instructional routine can be found in the

Ready Classroom program by Curriculum Associates. An earlier version of the curriculum included a regular lesson feature called Picture It and Model It that introduced students to new mathematical models and representations. We worked with the publisher to create the Try, Discuss, Connect routine that provides specific designs for interaction for students to analyze and discuss the models and representations and ultimately deepen their mathematical understanding. Do your curriculum materials have a similar regular feature or a repeating warm-up or wrap-up design around which you would like to build a reasoning routine?

You can start at different places, but in the end, there is a common process for developing a reasoning routine. In the next section, we share our process for creating a reasoning routine by starting with a mathematical practice, then connect that same process to starting with a common task type and a repeated lesson design.

A Six-Step Process for Creating a Reasoning Routine

Once inspiration has struck, we engage in a six-step process to create a reasoning routine. The process is cyclical, and the routine evolves and develops with increased clarity and purpose. The six-step process is summarized below and in Figure 5–1.

Step 1: Articulate the thinking goal for the routine. Ask yourself what habits or practices students will develop by engaging in the routine over time.

Step 2: Construct the flow of the routine. Lay out the steps or chunks of the routine. Ask yourself what process students could engage in that will position them to think in the ways reflected by the goal you identified in step 1.

Step 3: Build in designs for interaction between and among students and the mathematics throughout the flow of the

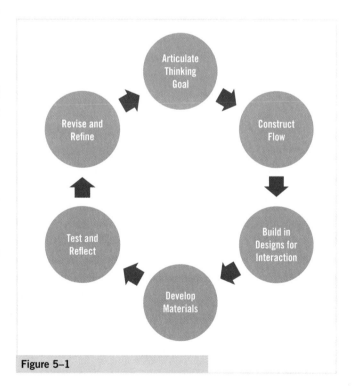

Figure 5–1

routine. Ask yourself where you will build in the essential strategies to ensure that you keep the focus on the thinking, step out of the middle, and support productive struggle.

Step 4: Develop materials. Find and/or create math tasks to sit at the center of the routine. Ask yourself whether the task invites the kind of mathematical thinking that is the goal of the routine. Create student-facing materials to support student engagement and teacher facilitation. Ask yourself what students will need to see and when they will need to see it. Will having a student handout increase or decrease student mathematical thinking and discourse?

Step 5: Test and reflect. Test-drive the routine multiple times with different tasks and groups of students to work out the kinks and reflect on its impact on students. Ask yourself whether all students were engaged and thinking mathematically.

Step 6: Revise and refine. Revise and refine the flow, designs for interaction, materials— maybe even the purpose—based on data from the test-drives. When implementation of your draft routine doesn't go as planned, ask yourself, *Is this a design or materials issue, or will the issue work itself out once students and I are familiar with the routine?*

As we unpack each of these six steps, we will connect them to our process as we designed routines you've read about (Contemplate Then Calculate and Decide and Defend) and our most recent routine, Analyzing Contexts and Models.

Step 1: Articulating the Thinking Goal for the Routine

Establishing the math thinking goal of the routine is a critical first step. A clearly articulated goal not only helps you communicate what the targeted mathematical thinking looks like to your students but also informs design decisions you make in each of the subsequent steps. Your thinking goal determines the AYQs and sentence starters and sentence frames you incorporate in the routine and drives the selection and creation of tasks that sit at the center of the routine. Lastly, you measure the efficacy of your routine against the thinking goal when you test-drive it.

Like mathematical concepts, mathematical practices are big, and reasoning routines typically zero in on just one aspect of a particular practice.

For example, we knew we wanted to develop a routine to target CCSS SMP 4, "Model with mathematics" (National Governors Association Center for Best Practices, Council of Chief State School Officers 2010). We started with the mathematical modeling cycle—analyze a phenomenon, formulate a model, compute with the model, interpret the results, improve and validate the model, and report results. This robust iterative process describes what a

mathematician is *doing*, but the question for us was, how are they *thinking* when they are doing it? What do they think is important to pay attention to? What are the questions they ask themselves that drive the actions they take? And which slice of that thinking do we want to target with the routine?

Although the modeling cycle itself is clearly defined, engaging in it requires deep mathematical thinking and reasoning. You draw on different avenues of mathematical thinking at different points in the process and when modeling different phenomena. For example, you reason quantitatively when analyzing the context or phenomenon to identify important quantities and use mathematical representations to capture the relationships between those quantities. Throughout, you attend to precision, as you make assumptions and consider the closeness of approximations. We zeroed in on one specific aspect of mathematical thinking for this first modeling routine, knowing we could create additional routines to develop other aspects of thinking driving the modeling process. We chose to focus the routine on quantitative reasoning because we felt being able to identify key quantities in the context under consideration was critical to choosing variables that would become the building blocks of the resultant mathematical model.

You cannot teach something you cannot name, and so, after identifying the specific math thinking goal, we work out how we will talk about the mathematical thinking with students. Our first pass at this comes in the launch of the routine when we describe *what* students will be doing and *why* they will be doing it. For example, we talk about structural thinking in the Contemplate Then Calculate launch by saying, "Find a counting shortcut by chunking, changing the form, and connecting to math you know" and "Think like the mathematician you are; use mathematical structure to find shortcuts."

Our first pass at working out modeling language in the Analyzing Contexts and Models launch included the goals "Consider the mathematics of a real-world situation, and analyze a model that represents the situation" and "Learn how to interpret the real world with a mathematician's eye and develop a bank of questions to ask yourself that are critical in the mathematical modeling process." Although both statements focused on modeling, neither addressed the quantitative thinking goal. We revised the goals to be "Learn how to interpret the real world with a mathematician's eye by focusing on the things you can count and measure" and "Understand how quantities and relationships from a context are represented in a math model."

Getting Started with Articulating a Thinking Goal for the Routine

1. Name the *kind* of thinking the routine will prompt and develop. You might start by choosing one of the CCSS mathematical practices or one of your state's math process standards. We find it helpful to do math with each other and colleagues and reflect on what we paid attention to and the questions that drove our math doing.

2. Get specific. What aspect of the mathematical practice or mathematical process standard will the routine target? Reread the mathematical practice or process standard and consider the various aspects of it.

3. Work out the language you will use to communicate the thinking to students. How will you describe the thinking to your students? We find it helpful to read what others have written about the mathematical practice and to also talk with colleagues to get a sense of the language they use.

Here are some questions to ask yourself when establishing the math thinking goal of your reasoning routine:

- What habits or practices will students develop by engaging in the routine over time?
- What would a mathematician notice when . . . ?
- What would mathematicians ask themselves when . . . ?
- What is the purpose or goal of this routine?
- Why should students engage in this routine?
- What will students learn by engaging in the routine?
- At the end of the routine, what do I want students to have learned?

Step 2: Constructing the Flow of the Routine

The flow of a reasoning routine is the sequence of steps of the routine that define what students will be doing. An effective flow sets students up to do the work of a mathematician. It engages students in a process that positions them to think and reason mathematically. Our reasoning routines follow a predictable flow: launch the routine, engage in a math doing process that prompts the thinking goal, share and discuss that thinking, and then reflect on what you learned about that thinking. For example, the process for Contemplate Then Calculate is notice, find shortcuts, and share and discuss shortcuts. In the Decide and Defend routine, students interpret the work, decide if it is correct, draft their defense, and defend their decision. These steps, like those in all our routines, are bookended by the launch, which clearly states the thinking goal, and the reflection, during which students name what they have learned about thinking.

Constructing the flow of Analyzing Contexts and Models meant revisiting the modeling cycle summarized in the CCSS (2010, 72):

- Articulate a problem

- Formulate a model

- Compute the solution of the model

- Interpret the solution and draw conclusions

- Validate and refine the model

- Report the solution.

Our goal was to choose a part or parts that would engage students in quantitative reasoning.

Quantitative reasoning happens at various points throughout the modeling cycle. You must focus on quantities (something you can count or measure) when you make sense of the context and interpret or articulate the *problem* to be solved. When *formulating* a model, you choose variables (quantities for which you do not yet have values) to include and build the model based on the relationships between those quantities. When you *interpret* your calculations and *validate* the model, you return to the context to make sense of your results; you consider if your results are appropriate values for various quantities in the situation. At this point you may decide that to improve your model, you need to consider other quantities or revise how you describe a relationship between quantities. One routine could not reasonably address all the places where mathematicians reason quantitatively in the modeling cycle, so we needed to narrow our focus.

We chose to focus the routine on three aspects of the modeling cycle: *make sense* of the problem and *interpret* and *validate* the model. These chunks seemed to be a reasonable size around which to build a reasoning routine as they would provide students ample opportunity to reason quantitatively, and the routine could be completed within one class period. We chose to omit the part of the modeling cycle where students create a model in favor of the parts where they reason about the context and model. We made this choice for several reasons. First, students do a significant amount of quantitative reasoning when they initially make sense of a context and again when they critique a model. Second, we have found that students view the model as the "answer" to a modeling problem and as such it often becomes an irresistible beacon that can eclipse attention to the thinking and reasoning. Lastly, focusing on creating a model can lead students who struggle to shut down because they don't know where to begin. Experience tells us that first positioning students receptively, in this case by interpreting and analyzing a model, builds their capacity and confidence to create a model.

We decided to present students with a real-world problem to analyze. We then asked them to make sense of the question being asked in that problem and identify aspects of the context to consider to answer the question (quantities and relationships). Then, instead of asking students to create a model, we gave them an improvable model and asked them to interpret it, decide how well the model addressed the question, and adapt the model as necessary. Asking students to interrogate and adapt the model positioned them to identify the quantities and relationships it captured from the context and also consider if other quantities should be included in the model or if the relationships were accurately represented. We believed that if students developed their capacity to analyze contexts and models, they would be well positioned to create, interpret, and revise their own models. Our eventual flow thus became launch the routine, analyze the situation, interpret a model, analyze and adapt the model, and reflect on thinking (Figure 5–2). We will build out steps 2 through 4 of the Analyzing Contexts and Models infographic as we continue through the design process.

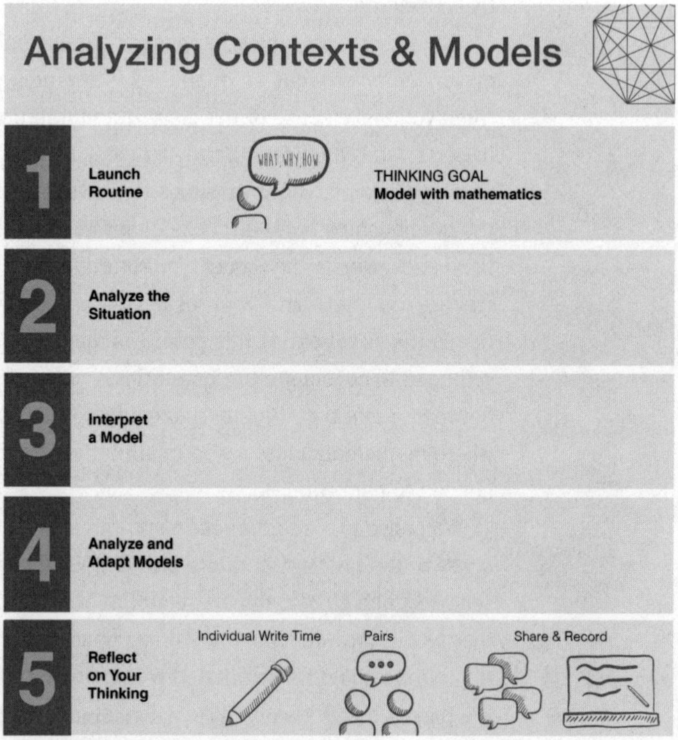

Figure 5–2

Getting Started with Constructing the Flow of the Routine

1. Identify what mathematicians do or what processes they engage in that require them to think and reason along the lines of your thinking goal. For example, if you are designing a reasoning routine to target SMP 3, you might think about the instances when you are "constructing a viable argument" or "critiquing the reasoning of others." These might include when you are crafting a proof, when you are making sense of or making the case for the validity (or lack of validity) of another's work, or when you are trying to convince others that your mathematical work is valid.

2. Double-check that the process in which you wish to engage your students is not too big. The process should provide students ample opportunity to engage in the thinking, but not take so much time that it can't be reasonably completed in one class period. We often begin by biting off more than students can mathematically chew in a routine. Recall that we focused on just three parts of the modeling cycle, leaving the other parts for another routine.

3. Determine the sequence of steps. Engage in the process yourself so that you can tease out the steps of the routine. We find that we always have an interpretation or sensemaking step, one or two steps to surface the thinking, and one or two steps to dig into and develop the thinking. We recommend no more than six steps, including the launch and final reflection. The names of your steps should describe what students are doing (e.g., analyze the situation, interpret a model, and analyze and adapt models).

Next are some questions to ask yourself when constructing the flow of your reasoning routine:

- What is the process in which I want my students to engage?
- Will that process elicit the thinking goal?
- What part(s) of the process do I want to include in the routine?
- How can I build that part/those parts of the process into the steps of the routine?
- Can the steps be reasonably completed in one class period?

Step 3: Building in Designs for Interaction

The designs for interaction you weave throughout the flow of your routine define how students interact with the content and each other. These include the foundational think-pair-share, the five essential strategies, and any specialized designs unique to this routine that increase engagement and make the mathematical thinking public. The designs define the routine's predictability and help us keep the focus on the mathematical thinking, step out of the middle, and position and support all students to think and reason mathematically.

Think-Pair-Share

The think-pair-share cycle is the foundational interaction design in our reasoning routines. We have found that providing students a small amount of individual think time to make sense of something tees them up to work constructively with a partner, which in turn provides them a space to work out ideas and language before full-group discussions where they will share their thinking and consider the thinking of others. Because it is a productive sensemaking design, think-pair-share shows up in our routines whenever students first consider a problem or representation or each other's work. For example, we use this design when students notice mathematically important features of a figure in step 2 of Contemplate Then Calculate and when they consider a classmate's defense in Part 5 of Decide and Defend. It is also a useful design for reflecting, and thus we end each of our reasoning routines with an individual write, partner share, and then full-group share and record. It is not uncommon for the think-pair-share cycle to be used multiple times throughout a routine.

Five Essential Strategies

The five essential strategies—annotation, AYQs, Four Rs, sentence starters and frames, and turn-and-talk—ensure a focus on the mathematical thinking and access for all students, so we think carefully about how we weave them throughout the routine. Here are some general guidelines for building in the essential strategies:

- Annotation: Use teacher annotation during full-group discussions and student annotation when students are interacting on paper with another's work. In both cases, the annotation is meant to highlight and make visible students' mathematical thinking.

- Ask-yourself questions: Use AYQs to help students orient when making sense of a problem, context, representation, classmate's work, and so on. We almost always use AYQs when prompting individual think time.

- Four Rs: Build the Four Rs into the design whenever students share and discuss their mathematical thinking in the full group. This will ensure you are stepping out of the middle and students are stepping up and making sense of and refinements to their classmates' mathematical thinking. In addition, there may be specific places in a routine where you want to publicly record student ideas or mathematical language for reference. For example, this happens in Contemplate Then Calculate when class noticings are recorded so that students can reference them when developing and discussing shortcuts, and the final step of all our routines when we share student learnings in the full group.

- Sentence starters and frames: Use sentence starters and frames to help your students organize and communicate their math thinking with a partner and in the full group. Always provide sentence starters and frames to students when they reflect on their learning.

- Turn-and-talk: Use turn-and-talk during full-group shares as an interaction structure for students to process and dig into mathematical ideas. Although sometimes turn-and-talks are spontaneous and responsive to class discussion, we do plan for at least one during each full-group discussion in our routines.

Specialized Designs

We often build in one or two designs beyond think-pair-share and the essential strategies in response to a particular avenue of thinking or a specific engagement goal. For example, a critical design feature in Contemplate Then Calculate is the initial "flash" of the object in step 2. We are purposeful about not letting the image linger because we want to stop and capture noticings. If the image is visible for too long, students quickly move to finding shortcuts and lose the initial thinking on which their shortcut is based. Thus, the flash is how we privilege the noticings. When building the designs for interaction into your routine, consider if there is an engagement, discourse, or thinking goal that might lead you to include a design element beyond think-pair-share and the essential strategies.

Building in designs for interaction is where you create the predictability of the routine and ensure that all your students engage in mathematical thinking and reasoning. It is also—we think—the most creative and fun part of building a routine!

After step 2, we had the basic framework for our modeling routine (see Figure 5–2). Now we needed to think about building in the think-pair-share structure, weaving in the essential strategies, and deciding whether there were any additional unique design features that we might include. We find that we always begin with the think-pair-share structure when building designs for interaction into our routines, and then we typically tackle the essential strategies. However, when we have a specialty design in mind that affects the architecture of the routine, we toggle between integrating essential strategies and the specialty design. The flash in Contemplate Then Calculate is an example of such a design, and we built that in before the essential strategies. On the other hand, a specialty design decision like having partners use different-color ink while annotating in Decide and Defend is less integral to the architecture of the routine and can be addressed after weaving in the essential strategies. When we were building the Analyzing Contexts and Models routine, we had a specialty design in mind that fell into the first category, so we solidified it before the essential strategies. (We'll say more about that design shortly.)

When considering the think-pair-share designs, we make decisions based on what students are processing and how much time and structure they need to process productively. It made sense to us that interpreting the question and context (step 2, analyzing the situation) should follow the think-pair-share sequence to allow students to steep themselves in the context. When students enter step 3, interpret the model, they need individual think time again to make sense of the model and time to share their interpretation and perhaps hear another interpretation from a partner. This initial sense making readies students to analyze and adapt the model and ensures that there are multiple interpretations in the class for a rich discussion in step 4. The analysis and adaptation of the model is a heavier lift that requires more time, multiple passes, and the multiple perspectives that a well-facilitated full-group discussion can provide.

The fun began as we considered possible unique elements. We had been seeing and hearing more and more about vertical nonpermanent surfaces (VNPS) and the positive impact they had on student engagement (Liljedahl 2021). VNPSs are erasable spaces—like whiteboards—on a wall or easels at which small groups work. With VNPSs students stand, collaborate, and share rough draft thinking. We were struck by the claim (Liljedahl 2016) that when VNPSs were used, student participation, discussion, and persistence increased—all hallmarks of a thinking classroom. We thought that making this feature available to students when they analyzed the situation (e.g., the amount of water all the students in this class will consume in their lifetime or if the cost to obtain a bachelor's degree from a private university is worth it) might increase both the quantity and quality of their quantitative reasoning. We still gave students some private think time to make sense of the question they were exploring and consider the context, but when they transitioned to partner work, we had pairs work together to record important quantities from the context on a VNPS. Working on VNPS provided pairs with an inviting space to share, discuss, and record a range of quantities based on their individual life experiences. The public nature of the VNPS and the openness of this step of the modeling process caused us to reconsider how the class shared after the partner work. The goal for the share-out was to have students consider different quantities and begin to think about assumptions embedded in identified quantities. Rather than have a full-group discussion, we decided to have partners tour three or four other VNPSs to see if those pairs considered different quantities or were making different assumptions about the context. Pairs then returned to their own list to reflect on and refine their work.

We decided to include another specialty design during the full-group discussion in step 4 of the routine. As partners shared their analysis and adaptations of the model, one student would explain the partnership's thinking while the other pointed to their projected work. We typically use the pointer and speaker roles when pairs share their thinking about a detailed visual, but in this case they were sharing the model they analyzed. The pointer and speaker roles not only ensure that partners present their shared thinking, but also help classmates comprehend what the pair is communicating.

With the think-pair-share and specialty designs for interaction set, the overall architecture of the routine was taking shape (Figure 5–3).

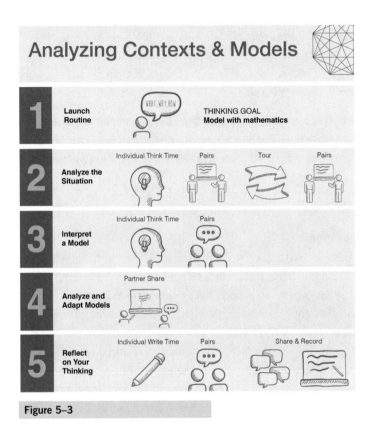

Figure 5–3

Step 1: The Analyzing Contexts and Models routine begins with an introduction to the routine, including a quantitative reasoning goal related to modeling with mathematics.

Step 2: Students steep themselves in the analysis of a real-world situation and related question. They begin individually by rephrasing the question and identifying what is important to consider about the context. Students continue as they stand with a partner and record important information that they know and that they'd like to know on a VNPS. They gain insight from other partnerships as they tour each other's workspaces and return to their own to edit, add to, or revise their ideas.

Step 3: Students work to interpret a mathematical model of the real-world situation that is provided to them. After some individual think time, they work with their partner to analyze its merits.

Step 4: Pairs assume pointer and speaker roles and present their analysis of the model in the full group. The teacher facilitates a discussion based on students' interpretations of the model and the class discusses how the quantities and relationships from the context are represented in the mathematical model, the assumptions made in the model, the limitations of the model, and/or how to adapt the model.

Step 5: Finally, students solidify all the reasoning they have developed during the meta-reflection process, as they reflect on their capacity to interpret contexts and models and how they might use it in future problems.

Next, we turned our attention to weaving in the essential strategies throughout the steps of the routine.

Annotation

We knew we would build teacher annotation into the full-group discussions, but we had to consider if students would be writing, and if so, whether student annotation would support their thinking. In this routine, students write at two different points: when they list important quantities, questions, and assumptions on VNPSs (step 2) and when they interpret the model with their partner (step 3). In the first instance they start with a blank surface (versus interacting with something already there) so they simply record their ideas. However, we decided to specifically prompt pairs in step 3 to annotate a paper copy of a model by labeling quantities, highlighting assumptions, adding questions, and so on. Doing so would ensure partners connected the comments their partners were making to the model, captured their thinking, and provided residue of the partner conversation when their work was shared and discussed in the full group.

Ask-Yourself Questions

We thought about the kinds of questions that would help students internalize their mathematical modeling, and in particular questions that oriented them to quantities and prompted quantitative reasoning. Since AYQs are particularly useful when first making sense, we looked to build them in when students were interrogating the problem context (e.g., "What's the question I'm exploring? What about this context do I need to consider?"), when they were considering what classmates had written on their VNPS (e.g., "Have they considered something we should also consider? Have they or we made assumptions?"), and when they were interpreting the model (e.g., "What quantities are included in this model? How are they represented?"). Our ultimate goal is for students to take these questions with them into their future math doing, so it is critical that the questions are productive.

Sentence Starters and Frames

We use sentence starters and frames to orient to the thinking goal and help students organize and articulate their mathematical thinking before sharing with a partner or in the full group. They often help students form their responses to an AYQ. In the case of the Analyzing Contexts and Models routine, that meant weaving sentence starters and frames into the following transitions:

- when individual students share their analysis of the context with their partner in step 2 (e.g., "Important quantities are _____"; "It would be helpful to know _____") and when the partners reframed and refined the quantities they captured on their VNPS (e.g., "The number/amount of _____"; "How many/much _____?")

- when individual students share their interpretation of the model with their partner in step 3 (e.g., "They considered the number/amount of _____"; "They found the number/amount of _____ by _____"; "A question I have about the model is _____"; "An assumption the model is making is _____")

- when pairs share their analysis of the model with the full group in step 4 (e.g., "We think the model predicts _____ because _____"; "We aren't sure the model is precise because _____"; "The estimation impacts the outcome because _____").

As always, we crafted sentence starters and frames to orient and support student's reflection on their learning at the end of the routine (e.g., "The next time I consider a situation and try to mathematize it I will ask myself _____"; "When thinking about constraints, it's important to_____"; "When analyzing models, I learned to pay attention to _____"; "A critical feature of modeling is _____"). We often craft more reflection prompts than we need and make decisions about which we will ultimately use when we test-drive the routine and consider student responses. You can read more about this in the revise and refine section later in the chapter.

Four Rs

We build the Four Rs into the routine primarily to help students process ideas and language during full-group shares. Thus, we built in opportunities for students to repeat, rephrase, and reword their classmates' thinking in step 4 when students share their analysis of the model and any adaptations to the model based on that analysis. We thought about whether to include sentence starters or frames that specifically prompted students to rephrase classmate's ideas (e.g., "They think the model predicts _____ because _____" and "They aren't sure the model is precise because _____"). We build in prompts like these if we worry that students will miss their classmates' thinking. Because the sentence frames students use to share their thinking in step 4 ended with the reasoning (i.e., filling in the *because*), we decided the thinking would be clear, and so we didn't need more sentence frames. In addition to prompting students to revoice each other's thinking, the teacher records relevant language during the discussion, as well as a sampling of student reflections at the end of the routine.

Turn-and-Talks

Since we use turn-and-talks to provide time and space—and sometimes another modality—to process ideas, we think about when students might need that type of processing support during a routine. In the Analyzing Contexts and Models routine students need that processing support in step 4 when they hear different analyses and suggestions about adapting the model. We also think about when we might be tempted to start explaining or teaching during a routine. We find that a turn-and-talk is a very effective move to take us out of the middle, and instead of answering student questions or explaining away student confusion, it provides students the opportunity to gain deeper insight and clarity with a partner. In the modeling routine, teachers are often tempted to step in and solidify student ideas around the model's precision, highlight assumptions the model makes, and/or suggest other quantities the model could incorporate. Thus, we built turn-and-talks into Analyzing Contexts and Models in step 4 when students share and discuss their analysis of the model to help teachers resist this temptation and instead shift the thinking work to students.

The Analyzing Contexts and Models infographic in Figure 5–4 illustrates the flow of the routine as well as many of the decisions we made regarding the essential strategies we just conveyed. Note the inclusion of annotation in step 3 and Four Rs, annotation, and turn-and-talks in step 4 of the routine.

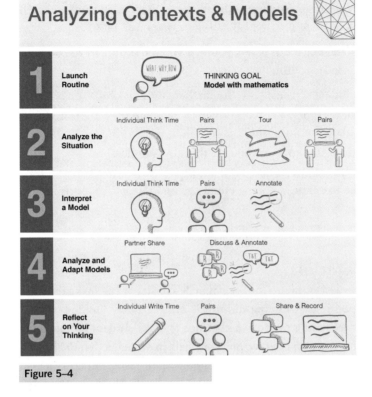

Analyzing Contexts & Models

1 Launch Routine — WHAT, WHY, HOW — THINKING GOAL **Model with mathematics**

2 Analyze the Situation — Individual Think Time · Pairs · Tour · Pairs

3 Interpret a Model — Individual Think Time · Pairs · Annotate

4 Analyze and Adapt Models — Partner Share · Discuss & Annotate

5 Reflect on Your Thinking — Individual Write Time · Pairs · Share & Record

Figure 5–4

Getting Started with Building in Designs for Interaction

1. Consider each chunk of the flow of your routine and how the think-pair-share cycle can support students as they make sense of the task and deepen and share their mathematical thinking. Sometimes one chunk may incorporate a complete think-pair-share cycle, while other times individual think time, partner work, and full-group share will span two chunks.

2. Consider if there is a unique design feature that grows out of a particular goal you might have (i.e., math thinking, engagement, or discourse goal) that you would like to build into your routine. We encourage you to be selective and choose no more than one. Keep in mind that students will engage in this routine regularly and the designs must keep the focus on keeping all students thinking.

3. Consider how to weave in the essential strategies to get and keep all students thinking and talking mathematically. Identify where annotation will support both full-group and partner discussions. Craft AYQs and sentence starters and frames to orient sense making and support sharing.

4. Keep in mind that the designs for interaction you choose are what is "routine" about your routine. Students will engage in them each time you facilitate the routine. Keep them purposeful: think focused, not fancy.

Following are some questions to ask yourself when building in the designs for interaction of your reasoning routine:

- How will students engage with the mathematics and each other?
- How do I slow students down to catch them when they are thinking and help them articulate that thinking?
- How will the design make students' thinking public?
- Where will I build in the essential strategies to ensure that I am keeping the focus on the thinking, stepping out of the middle, and supporting productive struggle?
- What other designs ensure access and engagement?

Step 4: Materials

Materials for our reasoning routines primarily consist of the tasks that sit at the center of the routines, an accompanying slide deck, and a student handout for the reflection. A subset of our reasoning routines makes use of other student handouts, though we are judicious about when and how we put materials in students' hands. In this section we will provide guidance on finding or developing math tasks and creating student-facing materials to support student engagement and teacher facilitation of the routine.

Tasks for Your Routine

The math tasks you place at the center of your routine spark the mathematical thinking. A task does not need to position students to engage in every aspect of mathematical thinking; however, it should not be so narrow as to force all students to think in exactly the same way. All our reasoning routines make use of a task that requires some initial sense making. Be it a worked example in Decide and Defend or a mathematical object in Contemplate Then Calculate, an effective task should invite students to notice and interpret with a mathematician's eye.

Tasks should prompt students to sniff out and relate quantities, or surface and use mathematical structure, or recognize and use repetition (i.e., prompt a mathematical avenue of thinking). Reasoning routine tasks are not about finding answers; they are about making representations, connections, decisions, and arguments. The task must provoke mathematical thinking, not answer-getting, and the thinking it provokes must align with the goal of your routine. For example, effective Contemplate Then Calculate tasks are mathematical objects (e.g., visuals, equations, graphs) that have structural elements worth noticing that facilitate the development of a counting or calculating shortcut. It doesn't matter if a worked example for the Decide and Defend routine is correct or incorrect; what matters is that it contains mathematics that students can critique based on mathematical reasoning versus a recalled rule or procedure or mathematical convention.

We recommend finding lots of potential tasks from a range of mathematical neighborhoods. Look through your teaching materials, texts, assessments, and other teaching resources. Amass a collection of tasks and then work on the tasks as your routine would have students work on them. As you work on them, reflect on if, when, and how they prompt you to think mathematically. Make sure you include a variety of tasks across a range of content areas so that your routine can be used throughout your entire curriculum.

When we began collecting tasks for Analyzing Contexts and Models, we looked through several textbooks, online resources like Three-Act Math Tasks, and modeling articles and resources published by the National Council of Teachers of Mathematics and other publishers. Looking over and working through the different types of tasks helped us clarify the kind of tasks that should sit at the center of the routine. Since students were analyzing and not developing the model in the routine, we could step away from more narrowly defined modeling tasks that targeted specific math concepts and representations. Because students would have to dig into both the context and the model within one class period, we tended to shy away from tasks that came with pages of data, tables, and graphics (or simply chose a slice of that data). We quickly became enamored with open-ended problems in which a student could gain traction by identifying relevant quantities, making justifiable estimations, and considering upper and lower bounds, in familiar contexts that they could quickly sink their teeth into: How many square inches of pizza will everyone in this classroom eat in their lifetime? What is the total number of snaps all the students in this class send in a week on Snapchat? What is the volume of air you breathe in one day? What is the total number of hairs on your head? Problems like these are perfect fodder for the Analyzing Contexts and Models routine.

We began reading the paper and scanning social media with a new set of eyes, noticing interesting contexts, questions, and models seemingly everywhere, and these became seedlings of modeling tasks. Current events provide rich fodder for modeling tasks. In 2020, these questions became highly relevant to model: How far will germs travel in the air? How many people does an eighth grader come in close contact with in forty-eight hours? Most importantly, we reached out to colleagues to share their favorite modeling tasks.

Then it was a matter of choosing or creating a model that responded to the question for students to analyze. The model had to be good enough that students could identify relevant quantities and relationships represented in it, but not so precise that it did not invite revision (e.g., another variable to consider, a more precise approximation). Figure 5–5 is an example of a question "ripped from the headlines" and a model we mocked up for use with the Analyzing Contexts and Models routine.

Is the cost of college worth it?

According to the U.S. Department of Education, in 2012, the nationwide average salary for young adults with a bachelor's degree was about $47,000, while only $30,000 for those with a high school diploma.

www.collegefactual.com

Colleges & Costs www.collegefactual.com	Bunker Hill Community College	University of Massachusetts Amherst	Harvard University
Average net price per year (tuition, room, board and other costs)	7,243	21,396	15,561
Average total student loans	20,576	32,588	25,720
Average salary upon graduation with a bachelor's degree	35,100	51,400	89,700

Model to analyze

$$-4\left(\begin{array}{c}\text{average} \\ \text{net} \\ \text{price}\end{array}\right) + -\left(\begin{array}{c}\text{stud} \\ \text{loans}\end{array} + \text{interest}\right) + \left(\begin{array}{c}\text{income} \\ \text{upon} \\ \text{grad}\end{array}\right) \times 4 + \text{raises} \quad \underline{OR} \quad 30,000 \times 8 + \text{raises}$$

Figure 5–5

See https://www.collegefactual.com for statistics on college costs: https://www.collegefactual.com/colleges /bunker-hill-community-college/; https://www.collegefactual.com/colleges/university-of-massachusetts-amherst/; https://www.collegefactual.com/colleges/harvard-university/

Once you have a collection of tasks, try to create a list of characteristics of an ideal task for your routine. Some of the characteristics we found helpful to consider when identifying tasks for the modeling routine included a context that is meaningful or provocative to students, multiple quantities to consider, an invitation to find additional relevant data or information, estimation, and grade-level content. (See the characteristics captured in the questions to ask yourself when choosing tasks for Decide and Defend, p. 67, and Contemplate Then Calculate, p. 95.) This will help you find future tasks. You will get to a point where you see tasks for your routines everywhere.

Student-Facing Materials

Visuals

We strongly recommend using visuals whether they are slides, chart paper, posters, or some other mechanism to display your routine's thinking goal and designs for interaction. Not only do visuals communicate the predictable steps of the routine to students and provide cues to the teacher, but they are also indispensable vehicles for essential strategies like AYQs and sentence starters and frames. Consider the slides for Analyzing Contexts and Models in Figure 5–6. Note how the first two slides frame the activity for students by communicating what they will be doing and why they are doing it (the thinking goal), and how it will happen (the flow of the routine). Notice how the icons used throughout the slides provide visual cues to students (and the teacher!) about how they will interact with their classmates and the content at each step of the routine. We have found that the icons are a critical support for English learners because they pair images with verbal instructions, increasing understanding and promoting access to AYQs (slides C, F, I) and sentence starters and frames (slides E, G, J, K, L). Include them on your visuals so that students can see and hear these prompts when you pose them.

Visuals like the slides in Figure 5–6 communicate the designs of a routine to students. For that reason, we find that the process of creating them is always both iterative and instructive. We are forced to work out our instructions, how we communicate the mathematical thinking to students, and the wording of AYQs and sentence starters and frames. Our first pass always has too many slides with too much on each slide. In the beginning, we are just getting used to the routine and need more support for ourselves on the slides so we can remember the designs for interaction. We refine the slides when we test-drive them with students and different tasks. We will provide more detail about that in steps 5 and 6.

Step 1: Launch the routine.

Analyzing Contexts and Models

WHAT: Consider the mathematics of a real world situation, and analyze a model that represents the situation

WHY: To interpret and engage in the real world with a mathematician's eye. To understand how quantities and relationships from a context are represented in a math model.

A

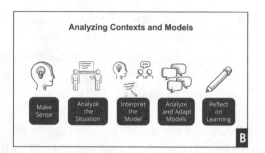

B

Step 2: Analyze the situation.

Make Sense of the Situation

Ask Yourself:

- What's the question I'm exploring?

- What about the context do I need to consider?

Insert Situation

C

Analyze the Situation

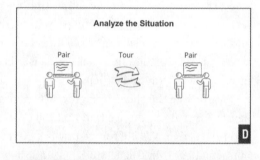

D

Share Interpretations & Analyze the Situation

Standing with your partner, share your interpretations of the context and together create a list:

- Important quantities are…

- It will be helpful to know…

Insert Situation

E

Consider Classmates' Interpretations

Tour the room and read others' lists. Consider what you'd add to your own.

Ask yourself:
- Have they considered something we should also consider?
- Have they (or we) made assumptions?

Insert Situation

F

Consider Classmates' Interpretations

Return to your chart, reflect and refine

- Place a + next to key ideas
- Place a - next to ideas less relevant
- Describe quantities as 'The number/amount of…'
- Articulate questions as quantities 'How much/many…?'

Insert Situation

G

Figure 5–6

Step 3: Interpret the model.

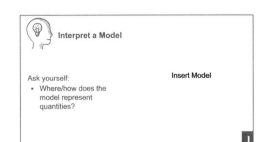

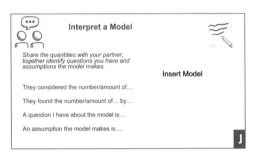

Step 4: Analyze and adapt the model.

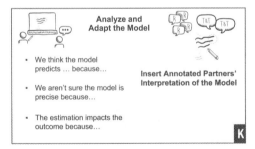

Step 5: Reflect on your thinking.

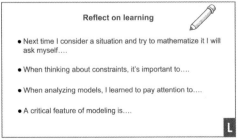

Figure 5–6 *(continued)*

Handouts

Since the goal of reasoning routines is to prompt, publicize, discuss, and develop mathematical thinking, we shy away from providing handouts to students. We find that when each student is given a hard copy of a task, student-to-student discourse immediately decreases and students' mathematical thinking is overshadowed by calculations and answers recorded on the page. Students tend to immediately jump into "doing" the math, recording results on the paper, and they slip seamlessly into sharing their solutions with partners, versus sharing their initial thinking and then working together *with* their partner on the task. For this reason, we create handouts only in cases where students have a great deal to process and interact with (e.g., a worked example in Decide and Defend), and then we always provide one handout per pair so students must work together. We also think carefully about when exactly students will need access to the handout. For example, we do not provide pairs the worked example handout in Decide and Defend until after the class has interpreted the problem and named what the work represents. Holding off ensures that all students are ready to dig into the analysis of the reasoning in the worked example with their partner when they have the paper in front of them.

There is one handout that we provide to every student, and that is the Reflecting on Learning recording sheet. The handout (or perhaps a Google Form or half sheet taped into student math journals or other vehicle for recording) contains the two or three sentence frame reflection prompts so that students can complete the frames without wasting time rewriting them. It also allows teachers to take in student reflections in real time to make decisions about which reflections to share with the whole class. Finally, it provides a learning record that students can reference in their future math work.

When we thought about handouts for the Analyzing Contexts and Models routine, we knew we wanted a learning reflection sheet and figured it would be likely that students would need a paper copy of the model they were analyzing. We decided to keep the presentation of the context and problem lean so that they could be projected for all to easily see, read, and consider. Students could reference the displayed task when pairs were working on VNPSs to unpack the context. It quickly became clear that pairs needed the model on paper in front of them as they worked together to analyze it, because interrogating the model meant interacting with it (i.e., doing some calculations and recording them, and adding notes and annotations). As is typical for us, we decided to give one handout per pair, to promote collaboration as partners work together to analyze the model (Figure 5–7).

Question: How many square inches of
pizza will all the kids in our
class eat in their lifetimes?

1. What is the average amount of pizza
   a student ate this week?
   2.25 slices based on class poll yesterday

2. What is average number of slices
   someone eats in their lifetime?   72?
   $2.25 \times 52 \times 75 = 8,775$ slices   75?
                                                  78?

3. How many square inches are in one
   slice of pizza?

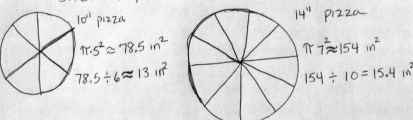

10" pizza

$\pi \cdot 5^2 \approx 78.5 \text{ in}^2$

$78.5 \div 6 \approx 13 \text{ in}^2$

14" pizza

$\pi \cdot 7^2 \approx 154 \text{ in}^2$

$154 \div 10 = 15.4 \text{ in}^2$

4. How many kids in this class? (26)
   $8775 \times 26 = 228,150$

$228,150 \cdot 13$
$2,965,950 \text{ in}^2$

$228,150 \cdot 15.4$
$3,513,510 \text{ in}^2$

$10 \text{ in} \leq x \leq 14 \text{ in}$
$78.5 \text{ in}^2 \leq x \leq 154 \text{ in}^2$
$13 \text{ in}^2 \leq x \leq 15.4 \text{ in}^2$
$2,965,950 \text{ in}^2 \leq x \leq 3,513,510 \text{ in}^2$

Figure 5–7

Figure 5–7 was inspired by student work found at https://morethanmath.weebly.com/fermi-problem-student-work.html.

Getting Started with Developing Materials

1. Collect lots of potential tasks. Make sure that the tasks you pick cover a wide range of content. Work on the tasks as you would have students do in your routine and reflect on your own mathematical thinking. Are you thinking in ways that align with your math thinking goal? If so, you probably have a good task.

2. Create visuals to hold the flow, designs for interaction, and task of your routine. Peruse the slides on fosteringmathpractices.com for ideas. All the slides for our reasoning routines have a similar look and feel; copy them or make your own. Whatever you choose to do, we recommend keeping a similar look and feel to the visuals you create for your routines. This will help students take up new routines.

3. Consider whether you actually need handouts. As teachers we are wired to give students handouts, mostly because they grow out of a legacy of practicing math skills and procedures. Developing mathematical thinking is different; it requires a lot less writing and a lot more sense making and discussion. Sometimes providing handouts to students can short-circuit that process.

Following are some questions to ask yourself when developing materials for your reasoning routine:

- Does the kind of mathematical thinking this task invites match the routine's thinking goal?

- What will students need to see and when will they need to see it?

- How and where will I build AYQs, sentence starters and frames, and other essential strategy prompts and cues into the visuals?

- How will materials affect student interactions? Will a handout or manipulative instigate thinking and discussion between students or will it lead to individual work and a focus on answers?

- Will having something to write on increase student mathematical thinking and discourse?

Step 5: Test and Reflect

Now that you've developed the architecture of your routine, test-drive it to work out the kinks. It is important to remember that you are not test-driving a discrete lesson, but rather a lesson flow with designs for interaction that will become routine for students. As teachers we are very adept at trying something new in our classroom once, reflecting on how it went, and then making a change for the next class or the next year. We approach testing and reflecting on the efficacy of a reasoning routine differently because of the repeated nature of the routine. Even the best-designed routine can be a bit clunky out of the gate while both students and teachers are getting used to it. Thus, we test the routine multiple times, either the same routine with the same task with multiple groups of students or the same routine with varying tasks with the same group of students each time. That way, we can determine if initial hiccups work themselves out as the flow becomes more routine. We constantly ask ourselves, *Is this an issue with the design of the routine or will it work itself out as we and the students learn the routine?* For example, when we first test-drove Contemplate Then Calculate with students, we worried that flashing the task might not provide adequate processing time for students. However, we test-drove the routine with the flash enough to realize that it provoked valuable noticings and prevented students from skipping the reasoning and jumping directly into calculations. In addition, as students became more familiar with the routine, they knew the goal of the noticing process and engagement continued to increase. We were thankful we didn't abandon this feature of the routine!

Capture as much data as you can when you test-drive a routine. We like to set up a video camera. It is also very helpful to have a colleague in the room taking low inference notes (describing what happens, not their interpretation of events) as the class unfolds. We cannot underscore enough how helpful it is to have another set of eyes and ears. If you are lucky enough to have both a human and a camera, train one on the teacher and the other on students. That way you can capture how the routine was facilitated as well as its impact on students. If at all possible, sit down immediately after the lesson and make some notes about your experience facilitating the routine and what you remember about students' thinking and engagement. Watch the video and/or read your colleague's notes and debrief with them. The closer this reflection happens to the enactment, the more powerful the debrief will be.

When you reflect on the data from your test-drive, begin by considering the impact on students' mathematical thinking and engagement and issues of timing. We find that starting with these wider angles naturally raises implications for the routine's math thinking goal, flow, designs for interaction, and materials. Figure 5–8 provides some suggested questions to ask and evidence to look for in each of the three focus areas.

We would be remiss if we didn't write about bringing students into the process. We encourage you to be open with your students about the fact that you are trying out the routine and that they are an essential part of the process. Ask them for feedback afterward: What worked, what didn't work, what was confusing? Have students complete a feedback form or convene a small focus group afterward, or simply have students tell you something they liked or didn't like about the routine as they walk out the door. However you do it, we strongly encourage you to enlist your students when you test and reflect on your routine. After all, your students have a vested interest in its efficacy.

Focus	Reflection Questions	Evidence
Mathematical Thinking	1. Does the routine prompt mathematical thinking and reasoning? Does the math thinking align with the routine's thinking goal? 2. Are all students thinking mathematically or just some? Who is thinking mathematically? 3. Did students take away what we hoped in terms of learning? 4. Does the residue of the discussion/student work/reflections connect to the thinking goal?	• Identify who is speaking and what they are saying both in pairs and the full group. • Write down what students say to their partners and in the full group. • Collect students' written reflections and any written work. • Take photos of annotated and recorded student work on the board, charts, VNPS, etc.
Student Engagement	1. Are students engaged? 2. Which students are engaged? 3. When are students engaged? 4. Who is doing the talking, the teacher or the students? 5. Are students using sentence starters and frames and the Four Rs when prompted? 6. When students turn and talk, does the classroom erupt or are there crickets?	• Track the number of students engaged in full-group discussions and partner work. • Note which students are engaged. • Note when students disengage and for how long. • Track the amount of time the teacher speaks and the amount of time students speak. • Note if students use sentence starters and frames and the Four Rs when prompted. • Note which students engage when prompted to work with a partner or turn and talk.
Timing	1. How long does each step of the routine take?	• Keep a running record of time spent on each step of the routine.

Figure 5–8

We test-drove the Analyzing Contexts and Models routine a few times with teacher groups before bringing it into the classroom. While working with a group of math teachers is not the same as working in the classroom with students, we find it helps us become more comfortable with the routine before facilitating it with students. We also find that teachers provide pointed feedback and ask questions that immediately get to the purpose of the routine and reasons for the design decisions we've made. Both inevitably help us clarify our language around the math thinking goal of the routine and refine the instructions. These one-shot opportunities to try the routine with adults also surface potential shortcomings that we can have on our radar when we facilitate the routine with students.

When we test-drove Analyzing Contexts and Models with students, we arranged to facilitate the routine with the same group of students three times and ran the enactments much like a learning lab. We asked the classroom teacher and two math coaches at the school to help us by filming the routine and taking notes. We asked each adult to focus on a different subgroup of students and write down what the students said. One of us facilitated the routine and the other recorded what the facilitator said and tracked timing. We printed out a copy of the slides and used them to record when in the routine the students and the teacher made comments. We gathered immediately after the lesson to reflect. We began by taking some individual time to read over our notes (and in the case of the facilitator, make some notes!), focusing on evidence of student math thinking and engagement. Next, we took turns sharing what we noticed (e.g., all student pairs talking and recording on VNPS, all students reading classmates' VNPSs when touring, students correctly interpreting symbols [π and x] they had not yet been formally introduced to in class, timing was spot on) and then shared any wonderings we had (e.g., will student use the AYQs to investigate other contexts? What would happen if the context was less familiar to students? When should we expect/prompt quantitative language? How do we help students annotate in a meaningful way?). Then we read over what students wrote when they reflected on their learning (e.g., "The next time I consider a situation and try to mathematize it I will ask myself: *What is the # of . . .* , *It would matter if . . .* , *It will be important to know . . .* , *What assumptions can I make?*, *What quantities or values should I consider?*" or "When analyzing models, I learned to pay attention to the precision of the information because it can create an imprecise picture of the problem, labels/quantities, what assumptions are being made and the impact those assumptions have on the outcome"). In this case, the student reflections were aligned with the math thinking goal, and thus did not give us pause or cause to make any changes.

While the reflection process may leave you wanting to make significant changes, we suggest that you test-drive the routine again before making any changes to the design. If you make changes after the first test-drive, and other changes after the second, and still more changes after the third test-drive, you will have in fact test-driven three different routines. However, you may want to make smaller, clarifying changes by adjusting language on the slides or tweaking processing time. Absolutely make note of potential issues after the first and second enactments, and focus your data collection on these trouble spots during your second and third test-drives. We will discuss the revision process in detail in the next section.

Step 6: Revise and Refine

After you test your draft routine multiple times and reflect on the impact it has on student thinking, engagement, and timing, it's time to revise and refine the routine based on any issues that arose. It is also not uncommon to make further refinements to your routine after subsequent enactments.

Revising the Goal

You may need to revise the mathematical thinking goal for your routine based on the breadth or depth of student's math thinking when engaged in the routine. For example, you may find that the routine actually prompts a narrower or even a broader aspect of the mathematical thinking than you intended.

When we test-drove the Analyzing Contexts and Models routine, it quickly became apparent to us that we were sending mixed messages around the thinking goal of the routine. When we reflected on the words we used to explain the purpose of the routine to students and the thinking prompts (e.g., sentence starters and frames, AYQs), we realized we were oscillating back and forth between focusing on the reasoning one does while modeling (e.g., talking about constraints and assumptions, "Develop a bank of questions to ask yourself that are critical in the mathematical modeling process") and specifically targeting quantitative reasoning (e.g., "Interpret and engage in the real world with a mathematician's eye by identifying important quantities in the context and identifying quantities in the model"). A similar thing happened when we test-drove the Decide and Defend routine, where we found a tension between focusing on the process of constructing and critiquing arguments and the type of mathematical thinking (i.e., quantitative, structural, and repeated) used in the argument. In the end, we found that the two could (and should) peacefully coexist and that it was a matter of which to foreground when facilitating. That decision is made by the teacher based on their goal for using

the routine. Similarly, we weren't yet clear on the exact goal for the modeling routine: Was it to develop the capacity to think quantitatively in the context of modeling, or was it to develop broader habits of reasoning specific to modeling? Because these two goals are not mutually exclusive, we decided it was a foreground/background matter, and we left it to the teacher to decide which to foreground. For example, if students have not yet developed quantitative reasoning, the goal focused on that will sit in the foreground. Once students are reasoning quantitatively, the focus can shift to the background and habits of modeling can be brought to the fore.

Revising the Flow

More often than not, we find we try to do too much in our routines. It is not unusual to only make it partway through a routine the first or even second time using it. This is because it takes more time in the beginning to explain the purpose and give the instructions, and transitions take longer because you and your students are not yet used to them. Once the predictability of the routine settles in, you move more quickly through it. If after three enactments you are still not getting through the routine, you are likely trying to do too much—or as we are fond of saying, you have more than one routine! If it takes more than a class period to complete your routine, consider jettisoning a chunk or streamlining the task that sits at the center of the routine.

Sometimes it is not that you have too many steps in your routine, but rather you are overindulging a particular step. This often grows out of having too many students share their work. In a thinking classroom, less is more. It is more productive to dig deeply into two or at most three lines of thinking, than briefly share and discuss five or six student approaches. Because this is a routine, students will engage in it many times and will have opportunities to share their thinking in future enactments. Tracking the timing of your routine when you test-drive can help determine if and where you are getting bogged down in the routine. Then the question becomes, do I cut a step out of the routine or spend less time in a particular step? We tracked the timing when we test-drove Analyzing Contexts and Models and found the timing worked, and so we did not need to make any revisions to the flow.

Revising Designs for Interaction

Lack of student engagement and the disengagement of certain students is often connected to the designs for interaction that you build (or neglect to build!) into your routine. If the data you collect point to a specific place in the routine where engagement drops, look first at the interactions you've designed (or didn't!) at that spot. For example, if you notice that students don't talk when they transition to partner work, this could be because there isn't enough individual think time prior to transitioning or that there isn't a sentence starter or frame to support pairs when they first turn to talk. If you observe engagement waning during full-group discussions, you may need to build in more annotation, Four Rs, or turn-and-talks to help students follow the discussion and process the ideas being discussed.

Often, we build in a unique design hoping to promote engagement, only to find it doesn't quite have the impact we imagined, and we need to tweak it. The VNPSs worked well in Analyzing Contexts and Models, as shown by students' immediate conversation about the context and copious recording of quantities and constraints. We were pleasantly surprised to see students' initial eagerness to take in classmates' ideas when they toured the VNPSs, but their interest decreased as the number of VNPSs they visited and the length of time they spent at each increased. In the end, we revised the tour expectations so that rather than visit every VNPS, students visited three other stations for a shorter amount of time, thus allowing us to make the most of the engagement boost of the design. In subsequent enactments we watched carefully to ensure that visiting just three stations provided students ample opportunity to investigate quantities, constraints, and assumptions they themselves hadn't considered.

When we first test-drove Analyzing Contexts and Models, we asked students to annotate as they shared their analysis of the model in the full-group discussion. We quickly realized that students were on overload as they attempted to share thinking that wasn't fully developed, communicate that thinking so that classmates could make sense of it, and capture essential ideas through annotation. As a result, we shifted the annotation role so that teachers annotate after students share their initial thinking and classmates rephrase it. That way, students still drive the discussion, and teachers support it through the annotation process.

After we test-drive the routine, we almost always find ourselves revising the AYQs and sentence starters and frames. When we first develop a routine, we craft more AYQs and starters and frames than we will ultimately use, because we want to test out which ones most effectively prompt the math thinking we are targeting. Often this decision is based on how students interact with the task in the routine and the prompts they naturally gravitate toward. We will include three or four different AYQs to support students as they make sense of problems, contexts, representations, and each other's work, and then look for the ones that gain traction. We also include more sentence starters and frames than we need to orient full-group discussion and reflections, and then zero in on the ones that bubble up as most relevant based on how students are thinking about the task.

In Analyzing Contexts and Models, we weren't completely sure the direction the full-group discussions of the model would take, so we included three different prompts ("We think the model predicts _____ because _____," "We aren't sure the model is precise because _____," and "The estimation impacts the outcome because _____") in our initial trials. Based on students' analysis of the model, we found ourselves gravitating toward the second and third prompts, but we were also left wondering how these prompts might change with different models. We kept this wondering in mind as we facilitated future enactments of the routine with different models.

Revising Materials

When it comes to revising materials, we mostly find ourselves streamlining our visuals. We inevitably include more slides and more on each slide than necessary, in part because we are learning the routine and need the visual cues when first facilitating it. We use two strategies to revise the slides to be less wordy:

- We use one- to three-word headings to communicate *what* students will be doing (e.g., interpret the context, share interpretations and analyze the context, consider classmates' interpretations).
- We use icons to communicate *how* students will be interacting (e.g., independently, with a partner, thinking, writing). We also reduce the number of AYQs and sentence frames once we've settled on the ones we want (see previous section).

If the task or worked example is complex, we often split it over two slides. For example, in Decide and Defend, we present the problem on one slide and then the worked example on a second, and in Analyzing Contexts and Models we share the problem/context first and then the model.

Continuously Refine Your Routine

You will find that you refine your routine with successive enactments by tweaking the language you use to describe the mathematical thinking as well as to give instructions. The more you talk with your students about the thinking goal and the more you see examples of the thinking, the more precise the language you use to describe it will become. When we first started facilitating Contemplate Then Calculate with students, we would say the goal of the routine was to "Think like a mathematician! Use mathematical structure to find shortcuts." After a while we realized saying "Think like a mathematician" sent the tacit message to students that they weren't mathematicians, so we changed our language and now say, "Think as the mathematicians you are." We also started to ask students new to the routine what they thought the word *structure* meant.

They gave great definitions like "the shape of things" or "how things work" and examples like "the framing of a house" or "the steel beams you see when a building is being constructed" or "the outline of a story." These images gave us more language to describe mathematical structure. When you have facilitated the routine enough so that the flow and directions have become routine, you will focus less on what you are saying and more on how you are saying it. This phenomenon promotes refinement without changes to the routine experience.

Starting with a Task Type or a Common Lesson Format

Whether you begin with a common task type or lesson format, you still work through the six-step design process, but you will have a head start on one or two steps. The lighter shading in the reasoning routine design cycle image in Figure 5–9 indicates where you will make fewer design decisions when starting with a common task type or lesson design. Designing a reasoning routine around a common task type will be an easier lift because you already have the task, a sense of the flow, and likely student-facing materials at the ready. Thus, it's a matter of identifying the mathematical thinking you want to target and articulating the designs for interaction. Similarly, a common lesson format such as

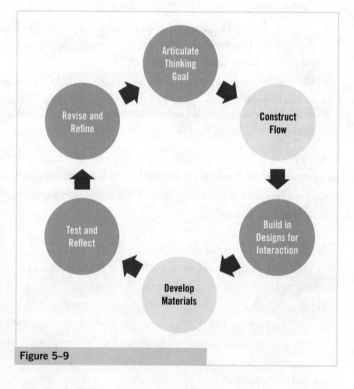

Figure 5–9

launch-explore-summarize that prompts thinking and reasoning also comes with many aspects of a routine already in place. The flow is well defined, the task is already determined by the curriculum, and there may be accompanying materials. Because the lesson format is used throughout the curriculum, the thinking goal you set for your students may be a larger grain size (e.g., making sense of problems and persevering in solving them [CCSS SMP 1] or constructing viable arguments [CCSS SMP 3] or modeling with mathematics [CCSS SMP 4]). Alternatively, the thinking goal may span a particular unit based on the content: quantitative reasoning during a unit on ratios, or structural thinking during a unit on equations and expressions. However, common lesson formats often lack specific repeatable designs for interaction of the kind we use. This is where you will need to place the bulk of your attention. Following are some AYQs to consider when transforming a common task type or lesson format into a reasoning routine:

- What about this task type or lesson format invites thinking and reasoning mathematically?
- What avenue or aspect of mathematical thinking can you surface, highlight, and develop with the task type or through the big ideas of a unit?
- What designs will orient students to the thinking and reasoning?
- What designs will ensure that students articulate their thinking when they share?
- How can I leverage the think-pair-share structure to promote thinking and reasoning?
- How can I leverage the five essential strategies to ensure students listen to and work with each other's ideas?
- How can I build in the five essential strategies to ensure students have enough processing time?
- Is there a unique design that would increase student engagement?

No matter where you begin, you will still want to test-drive, reflect, revise, and refine your routine once it is drafted. We hope you enjoy engaging in this process as much as we have!

REFLECT ON YOUR READING

1. Now that we've pulled back the curtain on our design process for building reasoning routines, what insights have you gained about reasoning routines?
2. How does the intentional design of a reasoning routine support the three shifts in practice?
3. What inspires you to design your own reasoning routine?

Making the Essential Strategies a Routine Part of Your Practice

This chapter is all about getting comfortable with the five essential teaching strategies for a thinking classroom. It includes a set of concrete activities you can work through to make the essential strategies a regular part of your teaching practice. Although you can absolutely work on the activities in this chapter on your own, we encourage you to collaborate with colleagues. Partnering with another teacher, a coach, or a team as you work through these activities will not only provide you additional perspectives and insights, but also will help you build a supportive learning community and affect classrooms beyond your own. We will say more about collaboration later in the chapter.

Learning to Use the Essential Strategies Effectively

The essential strategies are the key to quality implementation of our reasoning routines because they provide access to a wide range of learners and maintain focus on the type of mathematical thinking a reasoning routine targets. The essential strategies are also concrete steps teachers can take to focus more attention on the mathematical thinking, step out of the middle of student problem solving and discussions, and support students' productive struggle. Because of this, we believe the essential strategies are the "drivers" of mathematics teaching for thinking, and so we focus there.

Choosing Your First Essential Strategy

We recommend developing one essential strategy at a time. Once that strategy has become a regular part of your teaching practice, begin mindfully cultivating another. At the end of Chapter 2, we asked you to choose the strategy you would first like to incorporate into your teaching. Is that still the one you'd like to start with, or has another essential strategy risen to the top of the list either because you see how it would support your particular students or because it aligns well with your teaching style, or perhaps it simply seems like the easiest one to master? If you are not sure yet (and even if you are!) we invite you to use the survey in Figure 6–1 to reflect on each essential strategy and identify one you would like to develop.

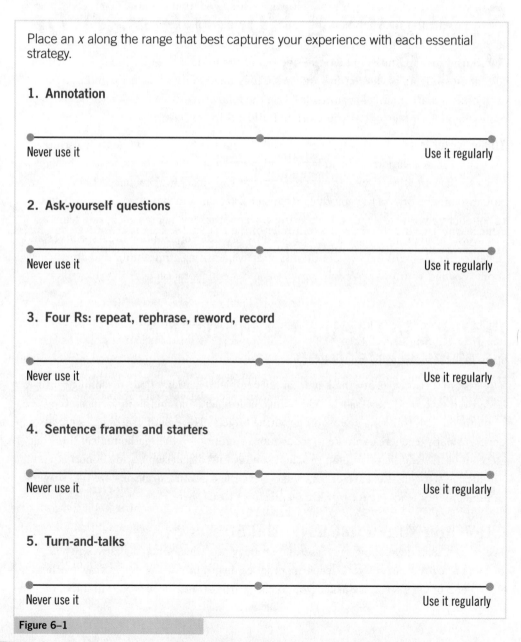

Place an *x* along the range that best captures your experience with each essential strategy.

1. Annotation

Never use it   Use it regularly

2. Ask-yourself questions

Never use it   Use it regularly

3. Four Rs: repeat, rephrase, reword, record

Never use it   Use it regularly

4. Sentence frames and starters

Never use it   Use it regularly

5. Turn-and-talks

Never use it   Use it regularly

Figure 6–1

Reflect on your responses to the survey in Figure 6–1. Which essential strategies would you like to work on? Which strategy would you like to tackle first? Why? How might the strategy help you place more emphasis on mathematical thinking, step out of the middle, and support productive struggle?

Articulating a Professional Learning Goal

We recommend articulating a professional learning goal that connects your chosen strategy to a particular instructional shift and reasoning routine to bring coherence and focus as you work toward a thinking classroom. An example of such a learning goal might be "I will use turn-and-talks to help me step out of the middle during Decide and Defend so that all students have the time and space they need to make sense of and critique each other's mathematical arguments." Use the following frame below to articulate your professional learning goal as you work to build a thinking classroom.

> I will use ____(insert essential strategy)____ to ____(insert shift)____
> during ____(insert reasoning routine)____ so that all students
> ____(insert impact on students)____ .

Your learning goal will serve as a reminder of the impact the essential strategy can have on your instructional stance, and more importantly your students' learning.

Learning Activities for the Five Essential Strategies

The essential strategies are an eclectic set of teacher moves. They differ in terms of their grain size and complexity, and the cognitive load on a teacher facilitating them has different origins. As such, the types of activities helpful for learning the essential strategies vary. Annotation, for example, requires responding in the moment to student thinking, and thus calls for activities that help develop the capacity to think on your feet. On the other hand, AYQs and the Four Rs are relatively straightforward in terms of process but call for actions (e.g., answering a question with a question or silence) that run counter to teaching habits that are second nature (e.g., explaining and showing or revoicing student ideas). Therefore, a critical step in getting comfortable with these two strategies is reflecting on your current teaching practice to understand how you typically respond. Finally, implementing sentence frames and starters and turn-and-talks typically doesn't require changing a deeply rooted teaching habit, but rather requires learning a multistep process, and so an activity like a rehearsal that allows you to work on the process of facilitating the strategy is called for. We have customized the following learning activities to target the unique demands of each of the five essential strategies.

Activities to Develop Your Capacity to Use Annotation

Annotation helps students "see" what their classmates are saying because it connects the words they hear to the mathematical representation about which they are talking. The challenge in annotating is that it takes place in the moment and is reactive to what students are saying, and often (especially at first) students communicate their thinking in less than precise language. It means you must listen carefully to what the student is saying, find the mathematically relevant idea in their communication, and then annotate it, making choices about the colors you will use and whether and how you will use words, symbols, numbers, and so on. And, of course, do all of this in real time. At first it can feel overwhelming. Fear not, with practice—and some preparation—you can become a masterful annotator. The following activities will help you build your annotating muscle.

Although annotation is knit into all our reasoning routines, it plays a central role in the Contemplate Then Calculate routine, and so we have chosen to situate the following activities in that routine.

Analyzing Annotation

There are any number of ways to annotate a student utterance; the most powerful are the ones that stay true to the student's thinking and keep a focus on the goal of the lesson. So let's try that. Consider the series of three annotations for each calculating shortcut in Figures 6–2, 6–3, and 6–4. Analyze each one and determine which of the three best represents the student's thinking while keeping a focus on the structural thinking goal. As you consider each one, ask yourself:

❏ Does the annotation accurately represent what the student said?

❏ Does the annotation draw attention to the particular structural thinking goal?

1. (Figure 6–2) **Structural thinking goal:** Chunk complicated objects to find counting shortcuts.

   Student counting shortcut explanation: "We noticed the 4 on top and the 3 groups of 2 on the sides, so we added 4 to the two 6s and got 16."

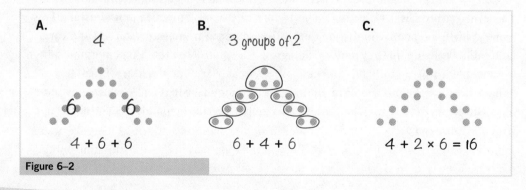

Figure 6–2

Let's start with what the student said. The explanation of their counting shortcut contains two types of information: what they were thinking (the words before the comma) and the resulting calculations (the words after the comma). It is the thinking you want to highlight with your annotation. For this reason, we dismiss C as it highlights the calculations and not the thinking. The annotations in A and B both attempt to connect the student's thinking to the structural thinking goal, showing the chunk of 4 on top and the same size chunks on each size they used to find their counting shortcut. Example A implicitly captures the chunking by placing the three addends near the parts of the visual they represent, but its focus on values shifts attention away from the chunking to the calculations. Example B visually emphasizes the chunking by circling the 4 on top and the 3 equal groups or chunks of 2 on each side. The color-coding in B invites students to see and connect visual and numerical chunks, setting them up to decipher where the 6s are coming from—a great question for a turn-and-talk! It is worth noting that the annotator in B also recorded the phrase "3 groups of 2," perhaps to underscore the chunking or tee up a structural connection to multiplication, or as a language support for the discussion, or all three!

2. (Figure 6–3) **Structural Thinking Goal:** Change the form of a mathematical object to make it easier to work with.

    Student calculation shortcut explanation: "We knew that 40% was just 10 away from 50%, so we took half of 35 and subtracted the 10% and got 14."

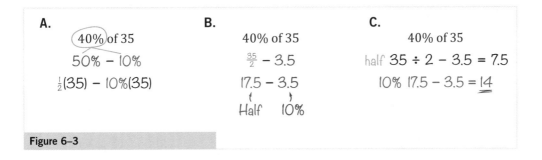

A.

40% of 35

50% – 10%

½(35) – 10%(35)

B.

40% of 35

$\frac{35}{2}$ – 3.5

17.5 – 3.5

Half   10%

C.

40% of 35

half 35 ÷ 2 – 3.5 = 7.5

10% 17.5 – 3.5 = 14

Figure 6–3

The structural goal in this example centers on changing the form of mathematical objects to make them easier to work with. In their explanation, the student changed the form twice. Did you catch both? The first was when they thought of 40% as being "10 away from 50%" and the second was when they "took half of 35." As is typical, the student did not clearly state, "40% was hard to work with, so I changed the form of 40% to 50% minus 10%" or "I changed the form of 50% to a half to make it easier to calculate." The structural thinking is hidden beneath the surface (and often to students themselves), so it is our job to surface and highlight it. Which annotation best makes this thinking public, while accurately representing what the student said? The annotations in both B and C clearly capture calculations (half of 35 less 10%), but neither underscores how the student changed the form of 40% and 50% to make their calculations easier. The annotation in A on the other hand shows that the student thought of 40% as 50% minus 10% by circling the 40%, writing "50% – 10%," and drawing lines to connect the difference back to the 40%. In addition, the annotator uses color-coding to visually connect the red 50% to the red $\frac{1}{2}$. In doing so they draw student attention to another instance of changing the form— 50% equals $\frac{1}{2}$. You could easily imagine the teacher posing a turn-and-talk prompt about the color-coded connections to help students process this idea of changing the form.

3. (Figure 6–4) **Structural Thinking Goal:** Find calculation shortcuts by connecting to math you know.

Student calculation shortcut: "The first thing we noticed were all the 5s and then we saw we could make a 5. Since it was all addition and we could add in any order, we did the 5s first and then added the 10s. So, 5, 10, 15, 20, plus 20 is 40 and another 40 is 80 and 30 is 110 and then the 4 is 114."

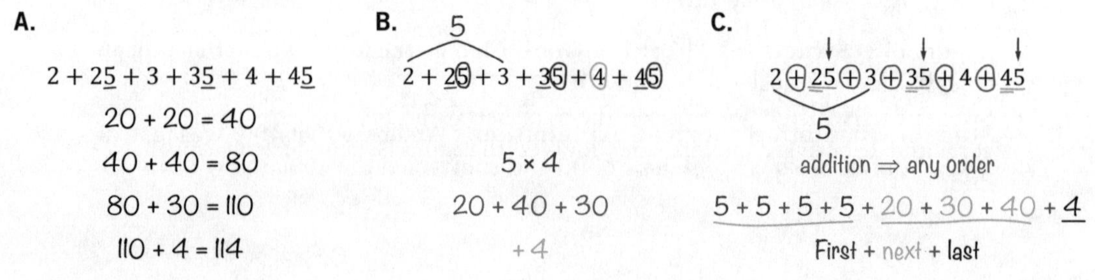

A.

$2 + 2\underline{5} + 3 + 3\underline{5} + 4 + 4\underline{5}$

$20 + 20 = 40$

$40 + 40 = 80$

$80 + 30 = 110$

$110 + 4 = 114$

B.

$$\overset{5}{\frown}$$
$2 + 2\textcircled{5} + 3 + 3\underline{\textcircled{5}} + \textcircled{4} + 4\textcircled{5}$

5×4

$20 + 40 + 30$

$+ 4$

C.

$2 \oplus 25 \oplus 3 \oplus 35 \oplus 4 \oplus 45$

$\underset{5}{\frown}$

addition $\Rightarrow$ any order

$\underline{5 + 5 + 5 + 5} + \underline{20 + 30 + 40} + \underline{4}$

First + next + last

Figure 6–4

In this example, the structural thinking goal focuses on how students make and leverage mathematical connections as they develop their calculation shortcuts. In this case the connections could center on the commutative property of addition, place value, and even the idea of multiplication as repeated addition. This powerful thinking is hidden beneath a lengthy and not yet fully formed student explanation, and the challenge is finding and surfacing it. This student noticed "all the 5s." All three annotations in some way highlight the 5s and can be leveraged to highlight the possible connections to place value or multiplication. Although the student doesn't provide a textbook definition of the commutative property of addition, they are clearly connecting to it when they say, "Since it was all addition we could add in any order." The annotation in C captures this mathematical connection by circling the addition signs and writing "addition → any order" and using blue ink for both to underscore the connection. The annotation in C also captures the mathematical connection to place value by highlighting the 10s in green. All three annotations use color, but the color-coding in sample C draws student attention to the mathematical connections that this student used to develop their shortcut, and thus the structural thinking goal of the lesson.

Practicing Annotation Offline

One way to broaden your annotating repertoire is to practice annotating student thinking several different ways and reflect on which most accurately captures the thinking and highlights your math thinking goal. This type of exercise is something you can (and should!) do when you are planning for an instructional routine. Figures 6–5, 6–6, and 6–7 show three sample tasks accompanied by student shortcuts that might occur in Contemplate Then Calculate. Think about the aspect of structural thinking you would like to highlight and write that down in the space provided for the structural thinking goal. Practice annotating the task multiple times. Reflect on the ways in which your annotation helps students see the structural thinking and how closely the annotation hews to the student thinking.

1. **Structural Thinking Goal:** _____

   Student thinking: "We noticed the symmetry and the columns of 2, so we got 6 and 1 more for the left side, doubled that, and then added the 2 in the middle."

Figure 6–5

2. **Structural Thinking Goal:** _____

   Student thinking: "We knew that 40% is $\frac{2}{5}$, and there are five 7s in 35, so 2 of them would be 14."

40% of 35   40% of 35   40% of 35

Figure 6–6

3. **Structural Thinking Goal:** _____

> **Student thinking:** "We noticed the pattern 2, 3, 4 and the 20, 30, 40 and that made us think of place value, so we added the 10s and got 90 and we added the 1s and got 5, 10, 15 plus 9 is 24, and just put the 24 and the 90 together, and got 90, 100, 110, 114."

$$2 + 25 + 3 + 35 + 4 + 45 \qquad\qquad 2 + 25 + 3 + 35 + 4 + 45$$

$$2 + 25 + 3 + 35 + 4 + 45 \qquad\qquad 2 + 25 + 3 + 35 + 4 + 45$$

Figure 6–7

Applying Annotation in the Moment

The best way to get comfortable annotating is to practice annotating in the moment. This type of thinking-on-your-feet practice helps you build your capacity to listen carefully to student utterances, make sense of them, connect them to your math thinking goal, and create visual residue that helps the rest of the class connect what they are hearing to what they are seeing and to mathematical thinking. As with any aspect of teaching that is responsive, you get better with practice. So, let's practice.

We are going to return to the same three Contemplate Then Calculate tasks. By now you are quite familiar with them and how they can be annotated to show student structural thinking. For this activity we will use the general structural thinking goal: *Think structurally by chunking, changing the form, and connecting to math you know.*

> **Remember not to annotate right away; be sure to have students revoice each other's thinking (for ownership) before you annotate. And always ask if that is how they were thinking about it.**
>
> —*DS, Grade 6 math teacher*

You will need a colleague or two to help with this activity. The colleague will first play the role of a student sharing a calculation shortcut and then play the role of another student rephrasing that shortcut. In the classroom, students often point and gesture while they talk and may correct or provide guidance if you are not annotating the part of the image about which they are talking. You can encourage your colleague to do the same.

Instructions

1. Prepare. Take some private think time to anticipate student shortcuts as well as how students might communicate and rephrase the shortcuts. Do not discuss this with your colleague so that when your colleague shares "student" thinking, it will be the first time you are hearing it and you'll be required to think on your feet.

2. Listen and point. While your colleague explains the student thinking, do not annotate. Instead, point (and gesture) to the aspect of the task about which the student is talking.

3. Annotate. Continue listening as your colleague rephrases the first student's thinking. Annotate *while* you are listening to the rephrase. When the rephrase stops, you should stop annotating.

4. Analyze your annotation. Together with your colleague consider how your annotating captured the student's structural thinking. (See Figures 6–8, 6–9, and 6–10.)

5. Repeat steps 1–4 with a second shortcut.

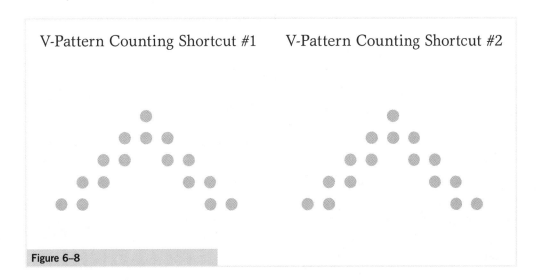

V-Pattern Counting Shortcut #1   V-Pattern Counting Shortcut #2

Figure 6–8

Percent Calculating Shortcut #1	Percent Calculating Shortcut #2
40% of 35	40% of 35

Figure 6–9

Sequence Calculating Shortcut #1	Sequence Calculating Shortcut #2
$2 + 25 + 3 + 35 + 4 + 45$	$2 + 25 + 3 + 35 + 4 + 45$

Figure 6–10

Video Analysis: Reflecting on Your Implementation of Annotation

It is difficult, especially at the beginning when you are working so hard to listen and make sense of student ideas, to remember after the lesson what students were actually saying and how your annotation unfolded. And it is nearly impossible during the lesson to also watch for the impact of annotation on other students. Video recording your lesson can help you capture both your annotation and its impact.

Video record your lesson, watch the section during which you were annotating, and reflect on how the annotation supported students as they shared and discussed each other's thinking. Start by positioning the camera so that it captures your annotation and picks up the audio of students speaking. After doing this once or twice, reposition the camera to record the class so you can capture their engagement with the annotation. It doesn't have to be anything fancy; the recordings are just for you to see and reflect on your annotating and its impact on students.

Following is a list of annotation "look-fors." We have broken the list down into student actions, teacher actions, and the annotation itself. You don't learn to annotate in one attempt; you build your annotation muscle over time. So, don't try to tackle the entire list the first time out! Here are a few suggestions for purposefully targeting specific look-fors:

- Pick a category to begin with: student actions, teacher actions, or the annotation itself.
- Self-assess. Read over the list of look-fors and reflect on your annotation practice. Select one or two you'd like to target.
- Collect some data. Record a lesson and watch it for evidence of all the look-fors. Consider the evidence and then select one or two look-fors you'd like to target.

Student Look-Fors

- Students see pointing and gesturing before the teacher annotates so that students have an opportunity to begin making sense of the idea.
- Students watch the teacher annotate as they listen to their classmates.
- Students refer to the annotation (e.g., the chunk in blue or the circled numbers or the term in the equation you underlined) during the full-class discussions.
- Students use the words and phrases included in the annotations during the full-class discussions.
- More students engage in whole-class conversations when the teacher is annotating than when the teacher is not annotating.
- Different students engage in whole-class conversations when the teacher is annotating than when the teacher is not annotating.
- Students start to make suggestions about what and how the teacher should annotate.
- Students start to annotate their own work.

Teacher Look-Fors

- The teacher does not annotate until students observe pointing and gesturing and the teacher is ready to accurately annotate the idea.
- The teacher annotates as another student rephrases or repeats the idea.
- The teacher annotates what the student is saying rather than recreating an annotation they practiced or prepared beforehand.
- The teacher stops annotating as students stop speaking.
- The teacher adds annotations as the math discussion progresses rather than trying to get everything down at once.

Annotation Look-Fors

- The annotation represents student thinking, not teacher thinking.
- The annotation focuses on the process and thinking, rather than the steps and the answer.
- Color is used to highlight and connect ideas, not arbitrarily.
- The annotation underscores and supports the lesson goal.

Even if you don't use video, you can always analyze annotation artifacts from your lesson. When you do, you will likely find that even though you may have used the same task with multiple classes, your annotation looks different across the classes. Just as discussions of the same math task vary from class to class, so will your annotations. If you have annotated the same task in four different classes and the annotation is the same, one of two things is happening: either you are annotating what you want to show and not what your students are thinking, or you have inadvertently led students to a common strategy.

Reflect on Your Learning

What have you learned about annotation? What aspects of annotation come naturally to you? What do you find challenging about annotation? How does annotation help you focus on thinking, step out of the middle, and support productive struggle?

Activities to Develop Your Use of Ask-Yourself Questions

AYQs can help you fight against the knee-jerk reaction to jump in and explain when students get stuck. They help you to step out of the middle, avoid taking over the thinking, and keep your students' struggle productive. Most importantly, when internalized, they become a mathematical compass that students can depend on when they don't know where to start, are stuck, or are spinning their wheels. Getting comfortable with AYQs means knowing what makes an effective AYQ, being able to craft an effective AYQ, having some back pocket AYQs, learning how to build AYQs into your lessons, and tamping down the temptation to tell and instead posing an AYQ. The following activities will help you develop these capacities.

Analyzing Ask-Yourself Questions

An effective AYQ has two qualities: it orients to and develops mathematical thinking, and it is neither too vague nor too specific so that it can be used across a variety of contexts and mathematical domains. With this in mind, consider the set of AYQs below. As you consider each question, ask yourself,

- ❏ Would they prompt students to think and reason mathematically?
- ❏ Could this question be used on a wide range of problems in a variety of mathematical contexts?

If the answer to both of those questions is yes, you've found an effective AYQ. Which ones do you think would be effective? Why?

1. How do I do problems like these?
2. What might be mathematically important about this situation?
3. How are these two quantities related?
4. Is this where I use (PEMDAS [parentheses, exponents, multiplication/division, addition/subtraction], butterfly method, and so on)?

5. Can I change the form of this to make it easier to work with?

6. Is this problem like the example in the book?

7. Will this approach work for any number?

8. What do I do here?

9. Can I represent this differently so that I can see what's going on?

Five of the questions in the preceding list are effective AYQs because they prompt mathematical thinking and they can be used across the mathematical landscape. They are questions 2, 3, 5, 7, and 9. Students asking and answering these questions will necessarily gain some traction into the problem on which they are working. Rather than cause students to think, questions 1, 4, and 8 position to students to recall or "do" something. Although question 6 may initially result in some reasoning about the similarities of two problems, the object in asking "Is this problem like the example in the book?" is to identify a procedure that can be activated to solve the problem, and not reason your way through a solution strategy. In addition, questions 4 and 6 have relatively limited use.

Practicing Crafting Ask-Yourself Questions

AYQs are particularly helpful for making sense of prickly problems, complex contexts, and mathematical representations; getting "unstuck" when problem solving; and drilling down into a mathematical concept. They orient students and prompt math thinking and reasoning.

Figures 6–11 and 6–12 show examples of classic incorrect reasoning about important mathematical concepts. Craft one or two AYQs for each example that would help students reorient to a more productive line of thinking without telling them how to think. After you have drafted your questions, ask yourself:

- Does the AYQ prompt mathematical thinking and not answer-getting?
- Does the AYQ only work in this instance or would students benefit from asking this question in other problem-solving situations?

A single serving of oatmeal is 3/4 of a cup. Aviva ate 1 cup of oatmeal. How many servings did she eat?

Matt's work

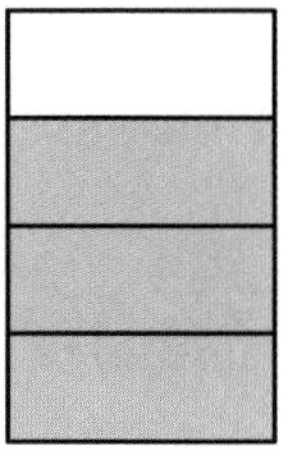

Since there is one 3/4 cup serving of oatmeal in one cup, and there is 1/4 cup of oatmeal leftover, Aviva ate 1 1/4 servings.

Figure 6–11

1. Write an equation to represent the following situation:
   a. Katie's age is 10 less than twice her cousin's age.

$$K = \text{Katie's age}$$
$$C = \text{Cousin's age}$$

$$K - 10 = 2C$$

Figure 6–12

An effective AYQ orients to and prompts thinking about important mathematics. In the case of the oatmeal example, the important mathematics is the question of the whole. Matt is interpreting the unshaded region in terms of the entire diagram (i.e., 1 whole cup of oatmeal) instead of interpreting the unshaded region as a fraction of 1 whole serving (i.e., the shaded region). AYQs that prompt thinking about the quantities and relationships in this situation will help reorient Matt. Some examples include "What quantities are represented in your diagram?"; "How are the quantities in the diagram related?"; "What do the shaded and unshaded regions represent in the problem context?" Remember, the purpose of the AYQ is not to prompt a correct answer, but rather to situate student reasoning in a fruitful mathematical neighborhood. With this reminder, let's look at the second example.

The work in the second example is typical of a student who is writing an equation by translating key words as they read from left to right, rather than interpreting the relationship between Katie's age and her cousin's age. Therefore, consider posing an AYQ that has students making sense of the relationship between the two ages. Two such AYQs might be "How can I re-present the situation with a diagram so that I can see the relationship?" and "How can I rephrase the relationship?" You'll note that we kept these AYQs as well as the ones we offered for the oatmeal problem general rather than problem-specific (e.g., "How can I re-present Katie's age and her cousin's age with a diagram so that I can see the relationship between them?"). While this may seem like an unnecessary layer of abstraction, it helps students see the utility of these questions across mathematics and not just as a "hint" for a particular problem.

Assessing the Need for Ask-Yourself Questions

Perhaps the biggest impediment to posing an AYQ is fighting the urge to respond to student struggle by telling or explaining. Understanding how you typically respond when students struggle is the first step to clearing a path for an AYQ. Video recording your teaching can help you determine how you typically respond when students struggle.

Video record one of your lessons, then watch the recording for times during the lesson when students got stuck, either because they struggled to make sense of a problem or arrived at a dead end or wrong answer while solving a problem. What did you do? Did you explain the problem to them, suggest an approach, remind them of a procedure to use, or ask a question that inadvertently told how to solve the problem? If so, then this is the perfect place for an AYQ. Take whatever you said or suggested and recast it in the form of an AYQ.

Watch more video of your teaching and take note of when you are inclined to tell instead of pausing and asking a question that will help students get themselves unstuck. Start anticipating these trouble spots in your planning and craft an AYQ or two that you can have in your back pocket if students get stuck.

Don't forget to reflect on your implementation of AYQs and the impact on your students. As you reflect, consider the following look-fors:

- AYQs were made visible for students to see.
- The teacher modeled the language of the AYQ.
- Students had individual think time to consider their response before talking with a partner or responding in the full group.
- The teacher referred to the AYQ when students were stuck.
- Students referred to displayed AYQs.

When reviewing the video, watch for any questions you find yourself repeatedly asking students. That repetition just may be an indication of a thinking habit your students need to develop; recasting your go-to question as an AYQ can help. For example, if you find yourself always asking students, "Have you defined your variables?" or "Have you labeled your graphs?" instead pose an AYQ that focuses on mathematical thinking like, "What are the quantities I'm relating in this equation or graph?" Lastly, make note of any time you could have posed an AYQ but did not. Reflect on why you did not use an AYQ and what you did instead.

Reflect on Your Learning

What have you learned about AYQs? What about using AYQs comes naturally to you? What is challenging about using AYQs? How do AYQs help you focus on thinking, step out of the middle, and support productive struggle?

Activities to Develop Your Use of the Four Rs

The Four Rs is a powerful processing strategy for students but can be deceptively difficult for teachers to incorporate into their practice. This is not because it is difficult to prompt a repeat, rephrase, or reword or to record math ideas and language; rather, for many teachers, the challenge lies in not being the ones who are doing the repeating, rephrasing, and rewording. If you have developed the habit of repeating and highlighting student ideas yourself, then your first step to use the Four Rs will be to break that habit. The first activity is designed to help you do just that. The second activity will help you to get comfortable prompting an *R*.

> **In effect, you are retraining student brains who initially respond to uncertainty by asking the teacher to instead respond to uncertainty by asking themselves the questions that can reveal a path forward. We thereby help students build the individual and collective agency to problem solve beyond the classroom.**
>
> —*CS, Grade 5 math teacher*

Assessing the Need for the Four Rs

If you have a habit of revoicing students' mathematical ideas or if you're not sure, this activity is for you. Video record one of your lessons. It doesn't have to be the entire lesson; you can start with a whole-class discussion. Watch the recording and take note of the times you restated something one of your students said. When and why do you tend to step in and restate? Do you repeat a student idea to be sure the rest of the class heard it? Do you rephrase the words to make them clearer? Do you reword student statements to model more precise mathematical language? Knowing when and why you step in and revoice your students' statements will help you know when to step out of the middle and ask one of your students to repeat, rephrase, or reword.

Choose one instance. Maybe you always repeat a student idea when it underscores the goal of the lesson. Then mindfully work toward prompting other students to repeat their classmates' on-point ideas. Or maybe you always rephrase students when what a student says isn't clear. Then remind yourself to have a classmate rephrase if a comment is confusing—or even if it's not!

We are big fans of talking with students about the importance of listening to each other, working to understand classmates' ideas, and working with each other's mathematical ideas. So, talk with your students about this shift from you revoicing to having them being the ones doing the repeating, rephrasing, and rewording. Take a moment and think about what you would want to tell your students about why you are implementing the Four Rs.

> Outside of the routines, I began to call on students to rephrase others' ideas, so I noticed students listened more attentively when their peers shared, recognizing that I wouldn't just summarize the important points for them. This helped shift the focus of the classroom discourse from centered on me.
>
> —KG, Grade 6 mathematics teacher

Video Analysis: Reflecting on your implementation of the Four Rs

After you start using the Four Rs, it is helpful to reflect on your implementation of them and the impact on your students. As you reflect, consider the following student and teacher look-fors:

Student Look-Fors

- Students listen to their classmates when they speak.
- Students repeat their classmates' ideas when prompted.
- Students rephrase a classmate's idea in their own words.
- Student rephrase adds detail to an initial idea.

- Students work to reword a mathematical idea when prompted by the teacher.
- Students refer to and use language the teacher records.

Teacher Look-Fors

- The teacher does not repeat, rephrase, or reword student ideas.
- The focus of the Four Rs is student thinking, not answers.
- The teacher reminds students that they will ask for a repeat or rephrase.
- The teacher holds students accountable for revoicing a classmate's idea and not talking about their own thinking.
- If students cannot rephrase a classmate's idea, the teacher, rather than doing the rephrasing, asks the original student to repeat their idea, and then asks for a rephrase.
- The teacher records important mathematical language for students to refer to.

Reflect on Your Learning

What have you learned about the Four Rs? What about using the Four Rs comes naturally to you? What is challenging about using the Four Rs? How do the Four Rs help you focus on thinking, step out of the middle, and support productive struggle?

I noticed...
so I knew...
so I looked for...
...connects to...
because...

Activities to Develop Your Use of Sentence Frames and Starters

An effective sentence starter or frame helps students organize and communicate their mathematical thinking. Additionally, starters and frames can be leveraged to support math talk between and among students. An example of an effective sentence frame used in the Contemplate Then Calculate routine is, "I noticed _____ so I _____." Getting comfortable with them means knowing when you have a good one, when it's a good time to use one, and how to use it well. The following activities will help you do just that.

Analyzing Sentence Frames and Starters

Consider the set of sentence frames and starters below. Which ones do you think would be effective? Why? As you ponder each one, ask yourself the following questions:

- ❏ "Does the starter or frame focus on mathematical thinking?"
- ❏ "Will it prompt a variety of responses?"
- ❏ "Is it stated in such a way that it is easy to use?"

If the answer to all three questions is yes, you've found an effective sentence starter or sentence frame.

1. Sentence frames to support students when sharing in class:

   A. "I did _____ and I got the answer _____."

B. "I knew _____ so I _____."

C. "When I saw _____ it made me think _____ so I _____."

The first sentence frame is not an effective one for a math thinking classroom because it prompts students to share what they did rather than how they were thinking. The remaining two sentence frames are designed to elicit thinking. Frame B prompts the student to start by sharing what it is they knew about the problem and how that led them to approach it. Like frame B, frame C prompts students to begin with their thinking, in this case what they noticed, but then further prompts them to share the sense they made of their noticing and then how that led them to approach the problem. All three sentence frames are easy to use in that both the structure of the frame and language being used are accessible. Lastly, all three invite a range of responses.

2. Sentence frames and starters to support students when analyzing another's work:

A. "They represented _____ by _____."

B. "I think their answer is _____."

C. "A question I have about _____ is _____."

The first sentence frame is effective because it prompts students to share their thinking (the connection they see between two representations) and is easy to use. Frame B is not effective because it prompts an answer and not student thinking. Frame C is easy to use and prompts mathematical thinking because it invites students to analyze another's work, consider a confusion they have about it, and reframe that confusion as a question.

3. Sentence frames and starters to support students when reflecting at the end of class:

A. "The next time I analyze visuals I will remember to ask myself _____."

B. "I liked this problem because _____."

C. "When I work on problems that have a _____ and I don't know _____ I will _____."

Sentence frame A is easy to use and prompts thinking because it positions students to articulate an AYQ and connect it to an aspect of mathematical sense making. Sentence starter B, although easy to use, does not position students to reflect on mathematical thinking. Sentence frame C is designed for students with an expected response in mind. This type of closed sentence frame often is both difficult to complete and does not prompt mathematical thinking.

It is worth mentioning in closing this activity that sentence starters and frames are not foolproof; even a well-crafted frame can produce an unintended response. For example, a student might respond to 2C by saying, "A question I have about their work is 'What's the last number on the left?'" or respond to 1C by saying "When I saw '$3x + 2 = 23$' it made me think 'algebra' so 'I got x equals 7.'" To minimize unintended responses, first make sure you use the sentence starter or frame to support discourse and reflection around math tasks that require mathematical thinking, and second, monitor student responses and reorient when necessary. The next activities will help you think about both of these implementation issues.

Building Sentence Frames and Starters into Your Lessons

When you plan, identify points during the lesson when students will be communicating their mathematical thinking, either to a partner, in the full group, or in writing. Those are the times a sentence starter or frame can be helpful. No need to overdo it; one well-placed sentence frame can go a long way.

Use this process to practice building sentence frames and starters into your lessons:

A. Pull out a lesson plan or a lesson in your text in which students are thinking and reasoning mathematically.

B. Identify the points in the lesson where students will be sharing and discussing their thinking with a partner or the full class.

C. Pick one point and craft a sentence starter or frame that will help them begin to share their thinking. Hint: Use one of the starters and frames in this book or *Routines for Reasoning* (Kelemanik, Lucenta, and Creighton 2016) related to the type of mathematical thinking students will be using.

D. Complete the starter or frame multiple times to ensure it is not cumbersome to use, prompts thinking and reasoning, and can accommodate a variety of thinking responses.

Rehearsing Sentence Frames and Starters

You can have the best sentence frame in the world, but students have to use it for it to be effective. The key to ensuring that your students use a sentence frame is purposeful facilitation. Start by explaining to students they all will be using the sentence frame or starter. You might say, "I'm going to have you start using sentence frames when you talk with a partner, because they will help you organize your thoughts and communicate your thinking, and in this classroom we place a premium on thinking." Use the following steps when introducing a sentence starter or sentence frame:

1. Project or record the sentence frame or starter, or provide it in writing.

2. Model the sentence frame or starter by saying it out loud.

3. Set the expectation that *all* students will use the frame or starter.

> Students are better able to have academic conversations with each other through the use of sentence frames. They learn to use those starters all the time and it leads to much better class and student-to-student discussions.
>
> —*HM, Grade 9 math teacher*

4. Give students some private think time to collect their thoughts, and then explicitly prompt the student(s) to share either with a partner or in the full group starting with the sentence starter or frame.

Practice by rehearsing setting up a sentence starter or frame. Move through each of these four steps and practice what you will do and what you will say. If you are able, video record and watch your rehearsal. Did you include all four steps? Were you happy with your wording? If not, try it again.

Video Analysis: Reflecting on Your Implementation of Sentence Frames and Starters

Once you start using sentence frames and starters, it's helpful to reflect on your implementation of them and the impact on your students. Revisiting video of your prior teaching without sentence starters and frames may help with this reflection. Did you follow the four steps for implementing starters and frames listed previously? What was the impact on students?

Sentence Starter and Frames Look-Fors

- Students used the sentence starter or frame.
- Using a sentence starter or frame when transitioning to a turn-and-talk increased the number of students talking with partners.
- Using a sentence starter or frame when transitioning to a turn-and-talk increased the amount of conversation.
- Using a sentence starter or frame increased the amount and clarity of student language production.
- Students communicated ideas relevant to the goal of the lesson as they implemented the sentence frame or starter.
- The sentence frame or starter prompted students to share their mathematical thinking.

Reflect on Your Learning

What have you learned about sentence frames and starters? What about using sentence frames and starters comes naturally to you? What do you find challenging about using sentence frames and starters? How do sentence frames and starters help you focus on thinking, step out of the middle, and support productive struggle?

Activities to Develop Your Use of Turn-and-Talks

Turn-and-talks provide students space and time to work out mathematical ideas and language during whole-class discussions. This processing structure is critical to facilitating meaningful math discourse in a thinking classroom. Turn-and-talks also provide teachers a concrete way to step out of the middle of class discussions and promote collaborative sense making among students. Effective turn-and-talks include something meaty for students to talk about, time for students to think before turning and talking, a sentence frame to orient and help students organize their thinking, and an indication of how much time they will have to talk with their partner. The following activities will help you get comfortable with turn-and-talks.

Analyzing Turn-and-Talks

Consider the following turn-and-talk prompts. Which one(s) do you think would be effective? Why? As you analyze each prompt, ask yourself, *Does the turn-and-talk prompt mathematical thinking and reasoning?*

Refer to Matt's work in Figure 6–11 on page 149.

A. Look at the unshaded region. Is the $\frac{1}{4}$ cup a quarter of the cup or a quarter of a serving? Think about that for a few seconds. Now share your answer with your partner. Use this sentence starter when you do, "The $\frac{1}{4}$ is a quarter of the _____."

B. Take thirty seconds to consider Matt's work. What connections do you see between the words that are written and the visual? Now turn and talk to your partner, and begin by saying " _____ connects to _____ because _____." You have one minute to discuss the connections.

C. Take a look at Matt's work and then turn and talk to your partner and tell them if you agree or disagree. Start by saying, "I think Matt's reasoning is _____."

D. So, some of you agree with Matt's reasoning and some of you disagree. So, turn and talk to your partner. How many $\frac{3}{4}$ cups are in 1 cup?

There is a lot to like about prompt A: it orients students to the crux of the problem in Matt's work, provides individual think time, and sets them up to reason. However, both the partner share prompt and the sentence starter focus on the answer and do not explicitly ask students to share their reasoning. Prompt B has all the components of an effective turn-and-talk prompt: individual think time, a clear question around something meaty to talk about, a sentence frame that prompts thinking, and a stated time frame.
Both prompts C and D have the makings of an effective turn-and-talk in that they center on agreeing or disagreeing with Matt's reasoning, but rather than focusing on analyzing

> With turn-and-talks more students get practice talking about the math, as everyone is an active participant of a conversation. As I circulate through the classroom, I'm free to listen in on students who are typically quieter in whole-class discussions, allowing me to encourage them to share their idea with the whole class, and enlisting their partners to allow them to practice before they share out. This enabled more students' voices to be included in the whole-class conversation, especially giving some of my girls and Black students more confidence to speak up.
>
> —KG, Grade 6 math teacher

Matt's reasoning, they focus on answers (i.e., agreeing or disagreeing and the number of $\frac{3}{4}$ cups in 1 cup). In addition, neither provides a time frame, and D lacks individual think time and a sentence starter or frame.

Practicing Crafting Turn-and-Talks

A great time to pose a turn-and-talk is when students get an incorrect answer and think they are right or when students have answered a question correctly and you want them to drill deeper into a concept. We've presented each of those scenarios next. Draft turn-and-talk prompts for each one. Make sure each includes all four characteristics of an effective turn-and-talk.

1. The wrong answer. Suppose you are working with your seventh graders on a standard related to "using variables to represent quantities in real-world problems and constructing simple equations to solve problems by reasoning about quantities." You ask your students to write an algebraic equation to represent "Katie's age is 10 less than twice her cousin's age." Most of the class falls into the trap of translating from left to right focusing on the numbers and key words, and craft the equation $K - 10 = 2C$ (as shown in Figure 6–12). Rather than explain why that equation is incorrect, you decide to pose a turn-and-talk prompt to provide all your students the time and space to figure out for themselves why the equation does not accurately represent the relationships between the ages of Katie and her cousin.

2. Digging deeper. Imagine your students have worked on the following task from the grade 7 Illustrative Mathematics program ("Discounted Books").

> Katie and Margarita have \$20.00 each to spend at Students' Choice book store, where all students receive a 20% discount. They both want to purchase a copy of the same book which normally sells for \$22.50 plus 10% sales tax.
>
> - To check if she has enough to purchase the book, Katie takes 20% of \$22.50 and subtracts that amount from the normal price. She takes 10% of the discounted selling price and adds it back to find the purchase amount.
> - Margarita takes 80% of the normal purchase price and then computes 110% of the reduced price.
>
> Is Katie correct? Is Margarita correct? Do they have enough money to purchase the book?

Most students have found the correct answer, that Katie and Margarita are both correct and that they have enough money to purchase the book. However, their justification is "Because I did it both ways and got \$19.80, which is less than \$20." Although you are happy that they were able to interpret the written explanations of the two strategies and could calculate accurately, you'd like to dig into the idea of seeing percentages as both an increase and a decrease of an original amount and maybe even identify the equivalent expressions. So, you decide to pose a turn-and-talk prompt.

Reread the turn-and-talk prompts you drafted. Will the question you asked result in students thinking and reasoning? Have you explicitly provided some individual think time and told students how much time they will have to discuss with their partner? Have you included a sentence starter or frame that will help students begin their conversation with their thinking and reasoning and not simply stating an answer or statement of agreement or disagreement? If the answers to these questions are all yes, you have crafted an effective turn-and-talk.

Rehearsing Turn-and-Talks

Much of what makes a turn-and-talk effective lies in how you facilitate it, so rehearsing is key. Use the following steps when introducing a turn-and-talk, and then pull students back together to share the fruits of their partner discussions in the full group.

1. Pose a clear question or prompt that will give students something to grapple with. Visually record the prompt whenever possible.

2. Provide some individual think time.

3. Provide and model a sentence frame or starter for students to use when they begin talking with their partners.

4. Tell them how much time they will have to talk together.

5. When you reconvene the class, remind them of the prompt.

Rehearse facilitating a turn-and-talk. Move through each of the five steps above and practice what you will do and what you will say. If you are able, record and watch your rehearsal. Did you include all five steps? Were you happy with your wording? If not, try it again.

Video Analysis: Reflecting on Your Implementation of Turn-and-Talks

Once you start using turn-and-talks, it's helpful to reflect on your implementation and the impact on your students. Review your lessons for times when you used a turn-and-talk. Did you follow the five steps for implementing turn-and-talks listed previously? What was the impact on students?

Turn-and-Talk Look-Fors

- Students talk with their partners when a turn-and-talk is posed.
- Students use the sentence starter or frame to begin their partner conversation.
- Student pairs discuss the prompt they were given.
- Use of the turn-and-talk increases the number of students ready to participate/participating in the subsequent full-group discussion.

- Use of the turn-and-talk increases the range of students ready to participate/participating in the subsequent full-group discussion.

- Use of the turn-and-talk increases the range of ideas discussed in the room.

Reflect on Your Learning

What have you learned about turn-and-talks? What about using turn-and-talks come natural to you? What is challenging about using turn-and-talks? How do turn-and-talks help you focus on thinking, step out of the middle, and support productive struggle?

Working on Essential Strategies Inside a Reasoning Routine

While you can work on implementing the essential strategies outside of a reasoning routine, we highly recommend that you leverage the routines in this book and in *Routines for Reasoning* (Kelemanik, Lucenta, and Creighton 2016) as you make the essential strategies a regular part of your teaching practice. The first and most practical reason is because all five of the essential strategies are thoughtfully built into their design and explicitly prompted in instructions and accompanying resources (e.g., slides and planners). The second and third reasons have to do with the nature of routines themselves.

The design of a routine does not change from one implementation to the next. This predictability helps you free up much-needed brain space, so you have more bandwidth to focus on the strategy on which you are working. Also, you can't develop a new teaching strategy in one lesson; you must work on it over time—especially if it requires reforming current practice. By definition, a practice is something you do repeatedly. Thus, the repeatable nature of a routine supports the ongoing attention needed to build a new teaching habit. Because you use a reasoning routine regularly, it sets you up to work on different facets of a particular essential strategy and reflect on and refine your use of it.

When leveraging a reasoning routine to develop an essential strategy, we recommend that you focus on one strategy at a time and follow this process:

When You Plan

- Identify where the strategy appears in the routine.

- Think about how it keeps the focus on thinking and supports the engagement of all students.

- Consider how it helps you teach into the three shifts: focusing on thinking, stepping out of the middle, and supporting productive struggle.

- Plan for the strategy (e.g., think through and practice annotating a task in Contemplate Then Calculate, or anticipate and craft the turn-and-talk question you will ask and the sentence starter or frame you will provide when digging into the arguments you anticipate students will make in Decide and Defend).

- Rehearse using the strategy.

When You Facilitate the Routine

- Focus on the essential strategy you are targeting.
- Share with students that you are working on the strategy and explain why it is important.
- Video record the lesson or ask a colleague or coach to take notes during it.

When You Reflect Afterward

- Watch the video or read over notes taken by a colleague and reflect on your facilitation as well as the impact on students.
- Use the previous look-fors to guide your reflection.
- Reflect on how the strategy helped you lean into one or more of the three shifts.
- Identify what worked well and questions you have.
- Articulate actions you took that you want to keep doing and one new action you will take as you continue to develop your capacity to use the strategy effectively.

Working on Essential Strategies with Colleagues and Coaches

The kind of change needed to transform math-doing classrooms into math thinking classrooms is not easy. It requires changing teaching habits, some of which are deeply rooted after years and years of teaching. Not only can working with colleagues and coaches offer more ideas and perspectives, it can help you create a supportive learning environment that will hold you up when the work gets hard, urge you on when the progress slows, and celebrate your professional development milestones.

Learning with a Colleague

We encourage you to work on the activities in this book with colleagues. Toward that end, we want to offer you some guidance on how to collaborate.

Try to do this with a colleague (a math coach if you have one) *or* videotape yourself and watch how much of the talking you do versus the students. I always learn more and more when having another set of eyes on my teacher moves.

—*DS, Grade 6 math teacher*

Analyzing activities are more fruitful when you can discuss your reasoning and consider alternative perspectives, so enlist a colleague or two and analyze the sample annotations, AYQs, sentence starters and frames, and turn-and-talks provided in the activities in this chapter. A natural next step is to share, discuss, and analyze the annotations, AYQs, and turn-and-talks you've crafted while practicing activities.

Ask a colleague (or coach!) to video record and/or take notes when you engage in a video analysis activity. Having a colleague do the recording will result in higher-quality video. They will also bring another pair of eyes and ears to take in data during the lesson and another perspective when reflecting with you afterward. Both are invaluable. The same can be said for when you rehearse prompting a sentence starter or frame or a turn-and-talk; having a colleague(s) watching with the look-fors in hand can help you spot places for improvement. Your colleague can also help you think through changes to make the turn-and-talk or sentence frame prompt more effective.

Professional Learning Settings

Leveraging routines for reasoning in professional learning settings with your colleagues allows you to jump right into the complexities of teaching mathematics together. When working with a common reasoning routine that holds so many components steady, you and your colleagues can immerse yourselves in mathematical content, students' conceptual development, and the teaching practices that will ensure all students develop as powerful math thinkers.

Many of the activities in this chapter grew out of the work we have done with grade-level, department, school, and district teams. We hope you will use them in yours. We have seen grade-level team members articulate individual professional learning goals and then work together to achieve those goals by leveraging a common reasoning routine and the essential strategies within it. We have seen math departments leverage the essential strategies and a common reasoning routine to articulate for students "what it means to do mathematics" and then work together to make the teaching shifts required to ensure all students were thinking and reasoning in their classrooms.

Following are two activities we use with professional learning communities: rehearsals and learning labs. Rehearsing a common reasoning routine or placing a familiar routine at the center of a learning lab allows everyone to focus on the teaching moves and the impact on student thinking, rather than spending time on how a particular lesson was designed or might be redesigned or taught differently.

Rehearsing Reasoning Routines

Just like actors rehearsing lines or running through a scene, rehearsing teachers can try and retry how they will facilitate a learning experience. Rehearsals not only allow you the opportunity to practice your lines, they position you to react in the moment to student thinking. In a rehearsal, if you are unsure what to do or don't like what you just said, you can stop, think for a minute, talk through the trouble spot with colleagues, and try again. A rehearsal is not teaching straight through a lesson and then getting feedback at the end. A rehearsal is all about learning in the moment. During a rehearsal everyone learns: the teacher who is rehearsing as well as the colleagues who are acting as the students.

We encourage you to use a department meeting, grade-level meeting, common planning time, or professional learning community time to rehearse your teaching practice with colleagues. You can start by engaging them in one or more of the mini rehearsing activities described previously that support the development of annotation, sentence frames and starters, or turn-and-talks. For example, you can practice annotating in the moment with colleagues playing the student role (i.e., sharing and rephrasing student thinking) while the rest of you practice annotating in real time. Share and discuss your annotations, and then switch roles. If you are working on a common reasoning routine with colleagues, rehearse the routine together. You might start by walking through the full routine and rehearsing the instructions and transitions simply to get used to the flow of the routine, then move to focusing on a specific essential strategy or shift.

Before you rehearse a routine with colleagues, it's important to be clear about why you are rehearsing and what everyone will be doing.

1. Set a rehearsal goal. Establish a learning goal for the rehearsal. Without one, nearly every move the teacher makes can be dissected, discussed, and practiced. The one rehearsing typically decides the goal by clearly naming what they want to work on while rehearsing (e.g., facilitating turn-and-talks that help students uncover the thinking underneath each other's ideas or stepping out of the middle and prompting students to repeat, rephrase, and reword each other's thinking). Establishing a clear goal will also help you decide if you should rehearse the entire routine or just the section(s) of the routine related to your goal.

2. Define the rehearsal roles. There are generally three roles that you and your colleagues will play in a rehearsal: the rehearser, the students, and a rehearsal facilitator. The rehearser is the teacher who is leading the group through the routine and working on a particular teaching move. It is their learning goal that drives the rehearsal. Everyone else plays the role of student. They engage in the routine just as the rehearser's students would. Ideally, one of your colleagues or a coach serves as the rehearsal facilitator. It's the facilitator's job to remind the group of the goal and roles and facilitate any discussion that takes place during the rehearsal. In a rehearsal only the rehearser or the facilitator can stop action. Colleagues playing student roles do not pause action, nor do they offer any advice unless the rehearser explicitly asks for them to weigh in. This keeps the rehearsal focused and the rehearser from being inundated with suggestions and advice. The facilitator

can use the infographic of the routine and essential strategy look-fors to help guide the rehearsal.

We find rehearsals to be incredibly powerful learning experiences. It is one thing to read about, think about, and plan to shift your practice in some way, but to actually have the opportunity to try out new teaching moves with colleagues who can say and do the things your students will, before walking into class, is an invaluable gift. Your colleagues are not simply doing you a favor by acting as students so you can rehearse; they will gain insights from the process as well. While they will see and reflect on the facilitation moves you tried during the rehearsal, they will also, acting as students, have the opportunity to dig deeply into how students might make sense of the mathematics and how they might communicate their thinking. Anticipating student thinking better prepares you to hear and respond in the moment.

Learning Labs Around Reasoning Routines

Unlike a rehearsal in which you practice the teaching move you are developing in the moment, a learning lab is a structure for anticipating, observing, and then reflecting on the execution and impact of a teaching move after the fact. It is a close cousin to analyzing classroom video together with colleagues and removes the limitation of the camera lens. You can run a learning lab with one colleague, a grade-level team, or an entire department. You are generally only bounded by the physical space in your classroom. A common reasoning routine is a tremendous asset when it comes to a learning lab, because everyone already knows the lesson plan. The routine sets the lesson flow, so you and your colleagues can jump right into the meat of the lesson: the mathematical thinking, how students will engage with it, and how the teaching moves will support their engagement.

Roles are straightforward in a learning lab: there is a teacher (or two coteachers) and there are observers. The teacher (and coteacher if there is one) leads the lesson and everyone else observes and collects data to support the discussion during the postlesson debrief. We find it helpful to set the expectation that observers do not interact with students, because doing so can often change the impact of the teaching moves (e.g., the students are asked to turn and talk to a partner, but instead of talking with their partner, a student engages with an observer; or a student gets stuck and an observer helps them, rendering an opportunity for the teacher to pose an AYQ useless). Instead, observers take low inference notes (recording what the teacher and students say and do, not their interpretations of those actions) as they collect data related to the learning goal of the learning lab.

A learning lab follows a predictable flow, and much like a lesson study or coaching cycle, has three parts: a prelesson session, the lesson itself, and then the postlesson debrief and reflection.

1. Prelesson Session. Before the lesson, meet with your colleagues and talk about the teaching practice goal (i.e., the essential strategy or shift on which you are working) and prepare for the lesson. This preparation can include working together on the math task at the center of the reasoning routine, anticipating what you will see especially as it relates to your teaching goal, and maybe even rehearsing part or all the routine. It is also important to talk about roles and expectations and articulate the kind of data you would like your colleagues to collect that will help you reflect on your teaching goal. For example, if the teaching goal is to use the Four Rs to step out of the middle and help students engage with one another's mathematical ideas, observers might track what the teacher does when a student shares their thinking, what a student says when asked to rephrase their classmate's thinking, or how the teacher responds when a student, instead of rephrasing a classmate's thinking, explains their own thinking.

2. Lesson. Talk with students about what a learning lab is, who the extra adults are in the room, what will happen, and, most importantly, why you are engaging in a learning lab. We often tell students that we teachers are working together to learn how to best help students learn to think mathematically and that the observers will be taking notes but will not be talking with students. Then the lesson continues as it typically would, with the exception of there being other adults in the room silently taking notes.

   Sometimes, during a learning lab lesson, the teacher finds themself at a turning point in the lesson, has a choice to make, and is not sure what to do. In this case the teacher (and only the teacher!) can call for a quick "teacher time out," briefly pause the lesson, and ask the adults in the room for advice. For example, the students may be considering an argument during the Decide and Defend routine, and the teacher wants to pose a turn-and-talk but is not sure which of two questions to ask, so she asks the observers. They quickly weigh in, the teacher makes the decision, and the lesson continues.

3. Postlesson Debrief. After the lesson, meet with your colleagues to reflect. Start with some individual writing time during which everyone can collect their thoughts; the teacher can jot down some notes and the observers can look back over their notes and highlight data relevant to the teacher's professional learning goal. After a few minutes, the group can begin to debrief the lesson. One possible process is to have participants write down things they noticed during the lesson and things they are wondering. Then, go around the room and everyone shares one thing they noticed. When everyone has shared one noticing, repeat until all the noticings are shared. Then do the same with wonderings. Once all the noticings and wonderings are shared, discuss trends and common questions. End the debrief by having everyone reflect on what they are taking away from the learning lab. Now would be a great time to schedule another learning lab and encourage a colleague to volunteer to be the teacher or to coteach the next one with you.

A few final thoughts on learning labs:

- Beyond a clear goal, roles, and a process, it is helpful to establish ground rules (e.g., don't interact with students or each other during the lesson, ground statements in observable data, be open to changing your perspective) for a learning lab, especially if this is a structure you hope to continue with your colleagues.

- Schedule the debrief as close to the end of the lesson as possible while ideas are still fresh.

- If you are working with a coach, invite them to participate in the learning lab as well. Coaches make great facilitators and are often more than happy to coteach the lesson.

Some Final Thoughts

We end this book where we started: all students must learn to think and reason mathematically. Making this a reality will require all of us to develop new teaching habits, and many of those habits will fly directly in the face of our current teaching practice.

We have watched many teachers introduce reasoning routines and the essential strategies into their classrooms. Here is what we know: it takes several passes before the routines feel familiar and a few more for the teaching moves within them to start to become second nature. But on the first pass, almost all teachers remark that students who typically watch from the sidelines are actively engaged in the lesson. This gives them—and we hope it will give you—the fortitude to try the routine again and keep working on the embedded essential strategies.

Working with your colleagues will not only help you in your efforts but will also go a long way toward increasing access and equity for all students. Working together, you can create a school where all students can expect to think and reason mathematically. Although this will not be quick work, it is essential, and we do not have time to waste. We must get started now.

References

Aguirre, Julia, Karen Mayfield-Ingram, and Danny Martin. 2013. *The Impact of Identity in K–8 Mathematics Learning and Teaching: Rethinking Equity-Based Practices.* Reston, VA: National Council of Teachers of Mathematics.

"Bunker Hill Community College Data & Information Overview." College Factual. Accessed July 9, 2021. https://www.collegefactual.com/colleges/bunker-hill-community -college/.

Danielson, Christopher. *Which One Doesn't Belong?* https://wodb.ca.

"Discounted Books." *Illustrative Mathematics Grade 7.* Accessed July 9, 2021. https://tasks .illustrativemathematics.org/content-standards/tasks/478.

"Harvard University Data & Information Overview." College Factual. Accessed July 9, 2021. https://www.collegefactual.com/colleges/harvard-university/.

Kelemanik, Grace, and Amy Lucenta, ed. "Fostering Math Practices." http://www.foster ingmathpractices.com/.

Kelemanik, Grace, Amy Lucenta, and Susan Janssen Creighton. 2016. *Routines for Reasoning: Fostering the Mathematical Practices in All Students.* Portsmouth, NH: Heinemann.

Lampert, Magdalene, Heather Beasley, Hala Ghousseini, Elham Kazemi, and Megan Franke. 2010. "Using Designed Instructional Activities to Enable Novices to Manage Ambitious Mathematics Teaching." In *Instructional Explanations in the Disciplines*, edited by Mary Kay Stein and Linda Kucan, 129–43. New York: Springer.

Lampert, Magdalene, Megan Franke, Elham Kazemi, Hala Ghousseini, Angela Chan Turrou, Heather Beasley, Adrian Cunard, and Kathleen Crowe. 2013. "Keeping It Complex." *Journal of Teacher Education* 64 (February 4): 226–43.

Lampert, Magdalene, and Filippo Graziani. 2009. "Instructional Activities as a Tool for Teachers' and Teacher Educators' Learning." *The Elementary School Journal* 109 (5): 491–509.

Liljedahl, Peter. 2016. "Building Thinking Classrooms: Conditions for Problem-Solving." In *Posing and Solving Mathematical Problems: Advances and New Perspectives*, edited by P. Felmer, J. Kilpatrick, and E. Pehkonen, 361–86. New York: Springer.

———. 2021. *Building Thinking Classrooms in Mathematics, Grades K–12: 14 Teaching Practices for Enhancing Learning.* Thousand Oaks, CA: Corwin.

Meyer, Dan. "Three-Act Math Tasks." dy/dan. Accessed July 9, 2021. https://blog.mrmeyer.com/category/3acts/.

Narasimhan, Swetha. "Fermi Problem Student Work." *More than Math.* Accessed July 9, 2021. https://morethanmath.weebly.com/fermi-problem-student-work.html.

National Council of Teachers of Mathematics. 2014. *Principles to Actions: Ensuring Mathematical Success for All.* Reston, VA: National Council of Teachers of Mathematics.

———. "What Is Notice and Wonder?" Accessed July 9, 2021. https://www.nctm.org/noticeandwonder/.

National Governors Association Center for Best Practices, Council of Chief State School Officers. 2010. *Common Core State Standards for Mathematics.* http://www.corestandards.org/wp-content/uploads/Math_Standards.pdf.

Nguyen, Fawn. "Growing Pattern 75." Visual Patterns. Accessed July 9, 2021. http://www.visualpatterns.org/61-80.html.

———. "Growing Pattern 116." Visual Patterns. Accessed July 9, 2021. http://www.visualpatterns.org/101-120.html.

Ready Classroom Mathematics (curriculum program). 2021. North Billerica, MA: Curriculum Associates.

Smith, Margaret, and Mary Kay Stein. 2018. *5 Practices for Orchestrating Productive Mathematic Discussions.* 2nd ed. Reston, VA: National Council of Teachers of Mathematics.

Stein, Mary Kay, Barbara W. Grover, and Marjorie Henningsen. 1996. "Building Student Capacity for Mathematical Thinking and Reasoning: An Analysis of Mathematical Tasks Used in Reform Classrooms." *American Educational Research Journal* 33 (Summer): 455–88.

Stein, Mary Kay, Margaret S. Smith, Marjorie Henningsen, and Edward Silver. 2009. *Implementing Standards-Based Mathematics Instruction: A Casebook for Professional Development.* 2nd ed. New York: Teachers College Press.

"University of Massachusetts Amherst Data & Information Overview." College Factual. Accessed July 9, 2021. https://www.collegefactual.com/colleges/university-of-massachusetts-amherst/.